NEXT STOP PLEASE

My Journey in Public Transport

Alan Scriven MBE

HEDDON PUBLISHING

First published in the United Kingdom 2023 by Heddon Publishing

www.heddonpublishing.com

A catalogue record for this book is available from the British Library

ISBN 978-1-913166-77-9 (paperback)

Cover Design: Heddon Publishing
All images contained in the book courtesy of the author.

This book is dedicated to all the people I have met as a result of joining the public transport industry, who have become good friends.

Prologue

The first thing to say is that this book is not a history of the public transport industry; I am in no position to write such a book. Rather, it is a review, if you will, of my considerable number of years in this crazy industry; a thirty-six-year career, during which I have occupied the positions of driver, driver-clerk, duty manager, traffic manager, garage manager, inspector, and assistant garage manager, in that order!

I am led to believe (but I may be mistaken) that King Charles II introduced the idea of public transport. He wisely considered, apparently, that the people should be able to travel about his kingdom at a fair price. And when quizzed about how the fares would be implemented, he allegedly said that it could be done in 'stages' with coaches pulled by horses; thus was born the term 'stage coach'. Bus travel by stages is still in operation today, and I think it works very well.

For me, it seems that buses have always played a part in my life, beginning at Woden Road Nursery, where I and my class of fellow four-year-olds were encouraged to have a short nap during the afternoons. We all had our own little foldaway bed, complete with motif at the head: mine was a red bus!

As a young lad, I would be on the buses quite regularly, as a passenger. The no.3 service operated between Fordhouses and Bushbury Hill, via Wolverhampton town centre. This route would take us to our school(s) in Park Village (we lived in Low Hill) when we could afford the fare; and also, when our meagre funds allowed, to visit our aunt Emma (who sadly passed away in 1964 at the very young age of just thirty-nine years old). She lived in Kipling Road, Fordhouses, with Uncle Harold and our Davies cousins, so we would get off at the Three Tuns pub (which is a Chinese restaurant today) and walk the rest of the way.

The alternative bus was the no.41. To get this bus, however, we had to walk from Fifth Avenue, Low Hill, to Bushbury Lane, boarding the bus outside the Railway Club. This bus took us along Fordhouse Road, as far as the Woodbine pub, and then we'd have to walk the few hundred yards remaining. Or we would just walk the whole way if necessary; it was not too far!

Our buses were green (livery) double-decker trolley buses, with a thin yellow band around the middle, and Wolverhampton Corporation Transport logo on the nearside. We (my siblings, our friends and I) were so used to the trolley buses that one morning whilst waiting for the bus for school, a 'half-cab' double-decker pulled up, and we refused to board it; going back home and telling Mom, 'The buses aren't running this morning.' Sadly, it soon became evident that the good old trusty trolley buses had had their day!

When alighting, we would challenge each other to jump off the rear platform whilst the bus was still moving. This somewhat dangerous caper eventually taught us that it was always left-foot-first when performing that manoeuvre. Always good fun, though.

Another challenge was to try and get a free ride. The conductors were usually on their mettle, to be fair, but very occasionally, by moving about from seat to seat and/or deck to deck, one could be on and off without having to pay for a ticket.

A lot of kids back in the 1950s and 60s collected bus tickets; some people still do. A friend of mine, and a colleague at Wellington Depot, Dave Skitt, collects *everything*, or at least used to. As does, I'm sure, our mutual friend and former work colleague at Select Bus Services, Dave Farrow.

The Wolverhampton bus depot was in Park Lane, as it still is today. The depot closed at one point, when the one in town near the Royal Hospital was used. In the fullness of time, this closed permanently, initially to become another car park. Today, however, residential properties take up the ground, giving Park Lane the opportunity to start up again. My son Tom worked for National Express (formerly Travel West Midlands) for ten years, and was based at Park Lane.

The bus station (much of the general public still refer to the station as the 'depot') when I was a child was in Thornley Street. It had a nice room within it for the bus men and women to enjoy their breaks, and it had a facility for delicious cooked food. I don't know if the public were 'officially' allowed entry, but no-one objected to me and my mates enjoying some chips in there after leaving the Saturday morning picture show at the Gaumont, the Odeon, or the ABC; whichever one we could sneak into... or possibly when we were lucky enough to be able to pay (even then, though, we would do our best to avoid paying if possible!)

Having completed a trilogy of books about a children's charity which I was a part of for thirty-three years, I wondered whether to give writing a break to concentrate on other things, and hobbies which I don't have a lot of free time for due to still working – on the buses, of course – full-time.

Speaking to a few friends, however, and colleagues and former workmates, more than one or two thought it might be worth writing about my considerable and varied career in public transport... and also to include some of their experiences. At the time of writing, I am working for Select Bus Services in Penkridge (South Staffs) as a driver. I was told in 2019, however, that in the 'near future', my work pattern would change. I was to become a 'show-up' of sorts, coupled with 'yard' duties.

The show-up duty means having to be the first driver to arrive at the depot. And if anyone missed their duty, or came in late, the person on show-up would start their duty. The show-up also meant that if everyone arrived for work, you could go home at about 1400hrs, because by that time most duties should have commenced. You had the option of finishing at 1400hrs anyway, even if you had to work a duty... or you could work the whole duty through (providing the person you were covering for didn't arrive within the first hour, because during the first hour it could be claimed back), thus earning a bit more for that day. In my experience, however, most people working the show-up duty preferred to go at the earliest opportunity.

I was well up for this new role, but for reason(s) never *really* explained to me, I was 'overlooked' (more on this later). I am therefore still driving at least forty hours per week. Yes, I could retire, but I don't see why I should, until I'm absolutely ready to, because despite having been overlooked, I am still enjoying working at Select. And I have to say, I am very happy now that I *was* overlooked.

My working career has not been wholly within the public transport industry. I had thought that I would be at Carvers – a Wolverhampton building merchants' – for all of my working life. It was my first job after leaving school, and I loved it. I started as a warehouse hand, at the same time as another lad, Keith Flavell. We worked alongside two older and experienced guys, Stan Wright and Danny Poole – two great characters – and we all came under the authority of the warehouse manager (the position I held by the time I left the company in 1976), Freddie Frith. The general manager was a Matt Busby lookalike by the name of Mr (Jack) Biddle; a wonderful man for whom I had great admiration, as well as a great man called Bill Williams[1], who has been the most influential male in my life.

I parted company with Carvers after eight years, however,

---

[1]You can find out more about this amazing man, and his fascinating life, in my three previous publications, about the Longmynd Adventure Camp: *The Longmynd Adventure Camp and Me; More from the Longmynd Adventure Camp and Me,* and *The Longmynd Adventure Camp and Me – The Final Chapter.* Published by Heddon Publishing, Wem, North Shropshire, and available on Amazon Kindle and from Amazon and most other bookstores in paperback.

because of the poor wages and the fact that my wife Tina had just given birth to our first son, Marc. I moved to Carvers' competitor, Ward Bros Ltd, but I only lasted twelve months there. I couldn't hack the immobility of sitting at a desk, answering a telephone all day; it was the polar opposite of what I had been doing at Carvers!

As a result of my leaving Wards, my then father-in-law secured me a position on the building maintenance team at Jenks and Cattell, the garden tools manufacturer based in Wednesfield, Wolverhampton. In my three years there, as a member of that great team, I qualified as a JCB 3C operator. However, I was unfortunately made redundant after three years, and from that point I drifted a little, doing various jobs to earn a crust before a serious football injury sidelined me for quite a considerable amount of time.

In putting this book together, I realised that for one reason or another there are situations and names that I cannot mention. That said, what I have included is an honest and true account of my years in the public transport industry, combined with a few light-hearted tales about people who, like me, are or were a part of what I will frequently refer to as this crazy industry!

As I said at the start, this is not a history of public transport per se, but an account of my experiences whilst being a very small part of it.

I hope you will enjoy reading it.

Alan Scriven MBE

I would like to offer my sincere thanks to all the people who have contributed to this book and to my publishers too, many thanks.

Chapter One

In the beginning

'A bus ride is like being in another world'
(J A Redmorski)

I was out of work in the autumn of 1986... but not for long.

I saw an advert in our local evening newspaper, the *Express and Star*. It said that the Midland Red (North) Bus Company was seeking to train people to be bus drivers, in order to join the industry. I wasn't even sure I could drive a car properly, but decided to apply anyway.

In response to my application, I received a letter which stated that the company was part of the National Bus Co. I was offered an interview by Mr L.A. Birchley (Fleet Engineer), pending my passing a driving assessment. A lovely bloke called John Perkins took me out in a minibus that I'm sure had enjoyed a previous life as a bread delivery van! John passed me, and an interview was arranged. I made the mistake of telling the interviewing panel about the back injury I mentioned in the Prologue. This was the reason, I added, for my current non-employment status.

The result of being so honest meant that I was asked to perform some silly exercise movements in order to prove to the interviewing panel that I was quite capable of sitting on my arse all day. That's how green I was, about joining the Red.

Shortly after the interview, a second letter from Mr Birchley popped through our letterbox. It contained an invitation to join the public transport industry... and the rest, as they say is history. I will do my best to explain what that has meant for me. Over the years, I have met some great people, many of whom have become friends. But alas, I have also come across some right bastards along the way... as you do!

My starting wage was £2.00 per hour, rising to £2.50 upon passing my Passenger Service Vehicle (as it was then called) driving test. We call it 'Passenger Carrying Vehicle' or PCV these days.

I passed the test first time, and after getting measured up for my uniform – complete with peaked cap – in Birmingham, I joined John Morrow's merry band of 'Noddy Bus Drivers' at a small outstation (actually a lorry park) on the corner of Bridgeman Street and Queen Street, in Walsall. The test came after a medical, which was a requisite of the position. The trouble was, no doctor could be found in time (before the actual test), so I and one or two others, including the now late Ken Parker (what a character he was) were taken to a veterinary surgery in Cannock, where the vet duly examined us... and passed us fit, after saying that we weren't actually barking mad to be joining the public transport sector!

Ken was kind enough to pick me up from home every workday morning, and we became good friends. He lived with 'the bride', as he always referred to his wife, near his local pub, The Gun Maker's Arms in Bradmore, Wolverhampton. A small, slight bloke, I guess in his mid-fifties, with a good head of hair that he took a pride in, Ken smoked Capstan full-strength cigarettes almost constantly... unless he was driving, of course!

Another driver I have fond memories of is Ernie Barnes; again small in stature, but with a cheeky grin which could 'disarm' anyone. He once talked me into appearing on the stage at Cannock depot's canteen in just a knotted shirt and a 'willy warmer', to present an award to one of the lady drivers. Not the kind of practical joke that would be allowed these days!

The company acquired a fleet of sixteen-seater Ford Transit minibuses, in a livery of red and yellow, hence the 'Noddy Car' name they were given by all and sundry. Proof of this came on the very first day I drove one in service. I stopped at a bus stop and opened the doors, so excited to have my first passengers: a young man with a small boy. I was deflated immediately, however; 'No thanks, Noddy, we'll wait for a real bus,' the gentleman replied with more than a hint of a piss-take.

That small outstation in Walsall, we all thought, would be there running out buses on three routes for years, because that is exactly what we were told. One of Morrow's driver-clerks, however, came across a letter left lying about in the traffic office. It contained confirmation that the depot would be closing in September 1987.

In March of that same year, my mother passed away, after a long illness; she had probably been living on borrowed time since 1983. A couple of days before she died, I was sat outside the 'depot' waiting to start the second half of my duty, when the reality that I was losing my mother (we had been given the sad news earlier by her doctor) got the better of me. I began to weep quietly, trying to hide it from the others. But one of the drivers, June Pretty, noticed me. She comforted me before going to Morrow and asking him to cover my work because she thought I should go home. I've never forgotten that nice gesture – thank you, June.

John Morrow was very good to me when I started at Midland Red, and I was always grateful. And when he eventually took over as Garage Manager at Wellington Depot, where I opted to move after Walsall closed, he continued to be generous; kindly allowing me use of one of the company cars whenever my own was off the road for a while – this was during the time I was commuting between Wellington and the flat I was living in on the Tettenhall Road in Wolverhampton, after my marriage had hit the rocks.

John also gave me my first Garage Manager position; back at

Cannock, in May 2000. But within the space of just three years, he managed to treat me unforgivably, twice: more about this dark episode of my career further into the book.

In spite of being lied to, with regard to how long Walsall Depot would be in operation, it was good fun whilst it lasted; we all enjoyed our time there. I was one of the first twelve starters, but our number had sufficiently increased by the time we commenced operating our services. One of our colleagues was a young lady whom, if memory serves, was called Val. John Morrow regularly had to correct her, and a few others, after hearing them referring to the buses as vans (which is exactly what they were, actually – converted Ford Transits). He was well blessed in the front teeth department, was John, and whenever he overheard the term 'van', he would vehemently hiss: 'They're bloody buses, NOT vans,' his teeth seemingly jumping from his mouth.

One morning, very early, during the late winter of 1987, with the depot still shrouded in darkness, John happened to notice someone fidgeting about on one of the buses. As he approached it carefully and curiously, the doors opened, and Val jumped out, giving Morrow a real fright!

'What the hell you doing, Val?' he asked loudly, scaring her as much as she had scared him.

'I had to change into my uniform, so I did it in the back of the van.' We all pissed ourselves laughing as John trundled off back to his office, shaking his head; great fun.

The three routes we operated were numbers 1, 2 and 3. The no.1 ran between New Invention in Willenhall, and the Yew Tree estate, via Bradford Place bus station, and the Delves estate in Walsall. Route no.2 offered a similar service to no.1, the only difference being that no.2 started its run from Ashmore Park, while Service no.3 ran a course from Walsall bus station to School Street, in Wolverhampton, serving Bilston and Darlaston en route.

The services were launched in a blaze of publicity; indeed, I featured on the pages of the local newspapers; in one, I was pictured with a young lady, the headline being: *Driving the girls crazy*. In another rag, a similar headline read: *MODEL SERVICE ON BUSES* and the sub-headline: *Drivers chosen for their personality*. Yes, I agree... they made a mistake with me!! These stories referred to my being pictured in a national newspaper previously, wearing just a pair of swim trunks and a smile.

The publicity blurb told how our services would use all available bus stops en route, but with the added bonus to the passenger of operating a 'hail and ride' system. I know I speak for many bus drivers when I say that this practice totally pissed us off! People would stop the buses anywhere and everywhere. And no matter how many times drivers tried to explain that this dreaded procedure had to be undertaken safely, meaning we couldn't just stop outside their houses, or any shop they wanted to go into, all we got in response was: 'Your timetable says we can do what we like.' Whoever invented the hail and ride system, I would wager, never drove a bus in service! It was a nightmare of the first order! And to be honest, there's been a similar system at every depot I've worked at, so I suppose I should be used to it by now... perhaps.

I remember driving the (hail and ride) 51 service around Arleston in Wellington. On this one occasion, I was rounding a left-hand bend when a passenger called 'Stop by that black cat, driver.' I thought, *Fuck this, I've had enough of this shit.* I approached the cat and then blasted my horn loud and long. The cat took off down the street with me in hot pursuit. 'Stop, stop!' shouted the lady. 'I'm trying to catch up with the cat,' I called back. Eventually, the cat jumped a wall and disappeared... so I stopped. The passenger alighted, calling me all the names under the sun, and threatening to report me, but I couldn't have cared less.

One of my colleagues at Walsall was a man called Bob Taylor; a great bloke who always had a story to tell anyone who would listen. Once, apparently, his bus was held up by a naked man standing in front of it and refusing to move... in heavy snow!

Whilst we were all still based at Cannock (waiting for the day when the Walsall 'enterprise' finally got underway after we had all passed the required test), us lads began mimicking a colleague by calling everyone 'chap', just as he did. I had a laugh with Paul Giles, who arrived in the second batch of would-be bus drivers destined for Walsall, over this. We quickly became friends, and I was asked to go out with him on his first day in service. On a miserable, wet morning, as we were coming down the road beside the Manor Hospital (Moat Rd, I think), there was a man running towards the West Midlands bus that was stationary at the bus stop ahead of us.

The local WM bus drivers got up to all sorts of dirty tricks in their efforts to prevent us making any progress; the company probably deemed that we had invaded their territory and, as one, the drivers decided to cause us as much hassle as they could, i.e. running just in front of us wherever our operations covered the same roads, and blocking us in at the Bradford Place bus station, whenever we had managed to actually get onto our designated bus stand. Contrary to popular belief, there's no 'honour' between drivers of different companies; we all do whatever we have to in order to stay ahead. The difference being that the longer you are in the industry, the more people you get to know. Drivers move between companies as the mood takes them (or for a wholly different reason), and this helps to form friendships... of a sort! So yes, you might well see drivers from different companies acknowledging each other with a wave, but generally speaking, there's no love lost if and when it comes to competition. And as for coach drivers; well, I have a few friends who opted to become coach drivers, rather than service drivers, including twin brothers Charlie and Denis McLafferty, Dean Davies and Kevin Bradburn, and at least one friend (Simon Harris) who drove coaches before turning to drive service buses. The usual rule of thumb in my experience, however, is they hate us, and we hate them (the aforementioned persons being the exception to the 'rule', of course).

On this first shift, with me accompanying Paul Giles, he was heading – he hoped - towards the first passenger of his career, and as he levelled with him, he opened the doors and shouted, 'Walsall, chap?' The bloke turned and eyed Paul momentarily, then missed his footing, and went arse over bollocks! As he did, the bus in front pulled away, giving Paul hope that his 'fallen prey' was destined to board our bus. Paul stopped, and smiled at the man, who was by now getting to his feet. 'Walsall, chap?' Paul repeated. The gentleman stood upright, turned to face Paul, and said, 'Fuck off, pal.' I was in bits; and almost pissed myself laughing as my startled and embarrassed mate closed the doors and pulled away, muttering, 'Miserable fucker, probably ain't had his oats this morning.'

From the very start, Paul Giles gave the impression (to me at least) of a ramrod-straight, no-nonsense type of guy. He would march around the depot (both at Walsall and later Wellington) going about his duties with a broad smile; a really great 'chap' whom you couldn't help but like. He went on to become an inspector for Travel West Midlands; or National Express as it is called today. I am still in contact with Paul (now retired) and his lovely wife Deborah, who has recently (as I write) had a very interesting and informative book published called *The Dog Always Cooks* (available on Amazon). It is a true story of a family member's fight against dementia, and Deb's part in that awful saga. I strongly recommend it.

Just after being let loose at Walsall, to do the job alone, Paul was getting towards the end of his shift. He had one passenger on board, but as he wasn't sure of the part of the route he was now on, he asked the passenger to guide him (always a big mistake, especially if operating a school service). He guided him, alright... straight to his front door, leaving Paul to negotiate a dead end!

On another occasion, Paul was a 'spare driver' one day at Walsall, so Morrow thought he would make use of 'idle hands'. He gave Paul a bin liner, and asked him to do a litter-pick of the whole yard. Ever the obedient servant, Paul waited around for about half an hour; then emptied the rubbish from the small canteen bins before taking his efforts to John for approval. Morrow congratulated Paul on a job well done!

Paul told me recently that he (like me and many others) loved his time at Wellington Depot, which I and a few colleagues and friends, e.g. Gurwinder Jandhu, opted for when Walsall closed. Eventually, however, Paul considered that there would be more scope for furthering his career at Travel West Midlands and with the benefit of time, I think he was right. Gurwinder (still a friend today) also migrated to TWM, along with a few others.

At Walsall Depot, we got on well with each other. We were all in the same boat; new to this crazy industry, so with no actual words being spoken (except 'chap'), we got stuck in, helping each other and doing our best for Morrow. And it has to be said that he in turn did his best for us. He was good to us all... in the beginning! It was a fantastic start to my career in public transport.

Christmas 1986 saw us all at Cannock Depot (because the new Walsall outpost hadn't yet got going in earnest). Most of the drivers there – excluding Tony Evans, whom I was destined to link up with again later at Choice Travel – and George Cox refused to even give us the time of day! No matter.

We were all neatly turned out in our Midland Red North uniform, complete with hat; or cap... if one chose to wear it, and our brand-new DD badges proudly sitting on our lapels. We bought each other Christmas cards (I'm not usually into that caper, but I joined in the fun) and to a man we wrote inside our cards to our colleagues, 'To chap, from chap.' Great fun. But it was all over in a flash!

We had all thought that we would be working out of Walsall

for the foreseeable future. We had our own fleet of new Ford minibuses; I and a few others had travelled to Folkestone with Morrow on three occasions to drive them back (one at a time) to our new depot, via Cannock, where they were all examined prior to service. But then, as I mentioned earlier, one of the driver-clerks showed us all a letter he had found in the office, stating that our depot would be closed down by September 1987! Morrow was asked straight out, by our depot union representative, regarding the validity of the letter. He offered a non-committal reply, obviously trying to keep the lid on growing anger and discontent! We had been duped! Apparently, it had always been the plan that Walsall would be closed down the following September, but we never found out why. As it was a condition of our employment that we joined the T&GWU, our union rep called for strike action, saying we had nothing to lose. Some of us agreed; a few didn't. But the effect was that hardly any buses went out on the following working day. Morrow called a meeting, and his smooth talk, combined with assurances that we would be okay regarding our continued employment within the company, was sufficient encouragement to convince us to get back to work. On 11th August 1987, however, I received the following correspondence from the company secretary:

Dear Mr Scriven

I regret to inform you that with effect from after duty on Saturday 05 September your position becomes redundant, and your services will no longer be required.

Your terms of employment entitle you to 1 week's notice of termination. Any outstanding holiday entitlement, and any redundancy monies due to you, will be paid to you at Cannock Garage on Thursday 10 Sept. If you have any difficulties with this please inform Mr J Morrow who will co-ordinate the arrangements. It may be that at other garages staff will be required, and if so, there is the possibility that this notice could be rescinded. In that event, you will be notified at once.

I wish to thank you for the service you have rendered in your time with us, and wish you the very best in the future.

So there was no actual assurance of continued employment as John Morrow had promised. However, at the closure of Walsall Depot, there was an opportunity to return to Cannock, or take a massive gamble on moving to Wellington. I took that gamble, along with – amongst others – Paul Giles, Gurwinder Jandhu, Ernie Barnes and Kenny Parker; moving from the 'Chaserider' badge of MRN to 'Tellus'. A few more names from back in the day at Walsall include John Yates, Vivien (alias 'Kermit') Charles, Dave Fryer... and Tanya Urquart, who also joined us at Wellington.

I was about to begin the best time of my life in the public transport industry, lasting for thirteen years!

Chapter Two

Wonderful Wellington

During my short time at Walsall, my wife Tina and I had split up, and I had moved into a small flat (more of a bedsit, really) on the Tettenhall Road in Wolverhampton. Luckily, Tina and I managed to stay on friendly terms, and this has stood the test of time; we have actually shared living accommodation on four occasions since our divorce in 1988. Our situation is the exception to the rule, I suppose! And I'm sure that our staying friends helped to make the transition easier for our children, Marc and Tom, to accept the circumstances.

I commuted between Wolves and Wellington until I was happy that I could settle at that old but wonderful depot. When I was sure, which was in the early part of the new decade, I applied for accommodation in Telford, and was lucky enough to be offered a two-bed ground-floor flat in Chiltern Gardens, Dawley, courtesy of Telford and Wrekin Council, which, I was told by my new colleagues, was in the business of quickly housing people who had moved into the town to work. It was very nice, and spacious, with a garage, front and rear garden, and in not too bad an area, as far as I knew. A few of my new colleagues lived in Dawley, including Kenny Rogers, Mick 'Buster' Edwards, Tim Clay, Ian Johnson, and Martin Bufton. So naturally I canvassed their opinion before accepting the tenancy. A short while after moving in, I was offered the opportunity to take a mortgage out on the flat, which I accepted. I had never seen myself as a property owner, but I considered it a good move that would hopefully pay dividends in the fullness of time.

Initially, Marc and Tom came for weekend stays. After a

while, however, they both got fed up with the travelling, and they missed their mates, so I went to visit them instead, whenever I wasn't working, and this arrangement worked very well. Later on, when Marc was older, he would come over on our 892 service (Wolverhampton to Wellington), sometimes with a friend - usually either Richard Hough or Kevin Wall - and, more often than not, they would have a walk up the Wrekin hill before catching up with me at Wellington bus station. On one occasion, a Saturday during deepest winter, Marc visited me alone. When it was time for him to leave, I put him on the coach that was operating on the 892 route, and off he went, after I asked him to get his mom to ring me when he arrived home. It had been snowing steadily for a few hours, but our buses continued to operate, so I went back to work. To my horror, however, when I returned to the depot at the end of my duty, my friend Debbie Ashford was waiting for me. She told me that the bus Marc was travelling on had been stuck in a ditch just outside Shifnal, for a couple of hours at least! I began to panic but Debbie proved to be a rock. 'Don't worry, Scriv,' she said, 'we'll go and get him.'

Dave Richards kindly looked after my cash-bag, promising that he would pay in my takings for me. Debbie and I jumped into her Mini and off we went to Shifnal in a raging blizzard! We found the bus; our friend Harry Singh was the helpless driver, still waiting for assistance. I boarded the coach and looked around for my son. He shouted, 'Dad I'm here!' before running down the aisle to me in an obvious state of relief. To this day, he says he was never happier to see me than on that cold winter's night. Debbie was brilliant; not only did Marc and I get into her small car but she somehow managed to squash in a total of eight people (including herself) and get us all safely back to either Telford or Wellington, to spend the night with family or friends.

On my first day at Wellington, I was greeted at the depot by Martin Bufton. What a great chap! Martin's job was to cover the duties (to me, the most difficult job in the traffic office), and he was brilliant at it. This particular position is one I am very grateful for never having had to do! I actually enlisted on a scheduling course (which included some duty-covering tasks) a little further into my career, and although I was told that I did well, that part of traffic duties wasn't for me. I was good at managing the drivers... although not everyone will agree with that statement!

Drivers would be in the canteen taking their breaks, when very often Martin, of average height, well rounded, with thinning 'salt and pepper' hair – probably in his mid-fifties at that point in his career – would waltz in and survey the room, always with a devilish smile on his likeable face, as he took his specs off. Then he would stroll up to his 'victim' and offer a sob story about being let down, and being 'in bit of a pickle'. Then he'd pounce: 'I want you to do this for me, cock, is that okay?' You just couldn't say no to Martin. After agreeing to do whatever he had asked of you, he would close with: 'Next time you're on show-up duty, I'll let you go early.' In reality, this hardly ever happened. His favourite saying on cold winter mornings was: 'It's nearly cold enough for a hairnet, cock.' Apparently, and certainly before my time, Martin got very inebriated at a company Christmas party, and 'sacked' everyone. And whenever he was asked about this, his reply was always the same: 'I started them all back on again on the Monday.' A real diamond was Martin Bufton; I am sure he was liked and respected by everyone.

The traffic office is the hub of the depot, and another very important aspect of running the office is to ensure that the morning 'run out' operates smoothly. The traffic officers need every driver to turn up for work in good time, allowing the driver to complete the 'first use check' of their allocated bus before taking it out. Also, there of course needs to be the required number of buses available. This can be difficult sometimes, due to buses being subject to an MOT appointment, vehicle inspection checks, sustaining accident damage, or perhaps a mechanical failure during the previous day.

The depot manager at that time was a good guy by the name of Geoff Venables (during my years at Wellington, the depot saw at least another four managers). Geoff welcomed us into his office to advise us, informally, on how the depot operated, etc. We were then taken on a tour of the premises, which I thought was very interesting, as it was a real old depot, with an abundance of history and character; built in the 1930s, I believe. Sadly, it was demolished some years ago to make way for... yes, you guessed right: housing.

The first shock I received at Wellington was being told by Martin Bufton that after some route-learning I would start my duties on the 'late rota'. It was nerve-wracking and strange for us new guys... until we got into it. I did, though, have cause to tell Mr Venables that I wasn't staying on late duties permanently, which I suspected Martin, bless him, thought, or hoped that I would. I did my share willingly, but I wouldn't let Martin take the piss! I think it's fair to say that most drivers weren't too keen on late duties. Starting work anywhere between 1400 and 1600hrs and finishing between 2300 and 0030hrs wasn't many drivers' cup of tea. And some (such as Tanya Urquart) would do anything to avoid them, even paying someone (George Bruck, usually) decent sums of money to swap duties. I did my allocated share, but found late turns boring; there would be hardly anyone on board, and few people in the depot at break times. One bonus, however, happened one evening just after pub closing time. I stopped at the Horseshoes pub in Ketley for a couple of young men, obviously the worse for wear after a few hours on the 'golden throat juice'. The first to board staggered past me, saying, 'He's paying, mate.' I thought, *Here we go*, but his friend got on and asked, in language I could hardly discern, the fare to Telford. I told him (I think it was about 90p each) and he fished a large handful of change out of his pocket and slammed it onto the cash tray; coins flying everywhere. 'Got enough there, mate, or do you need more?' He was swaying from side to side as I quickly surveyed the cash tray, and floor, before scooping it all up and dropping it in my cash bag. 'You're ten pence short, mate, but don't worry,' I replied as two single tickets issued from the Wayfarer ticket machine. The lads were no trouble, and got off the bus just a few stops later in Oakengates (perhaps with the intention of finding another watering hole). Counting my money at the end of my shift, I found I was almost seven pounds to the good. Nice.

Of course, some drivers actually preferred evening duties; the now late Peter Ashford (Debbie's father) being one, at least whilst he worked on renovating his home on The Rock estate, near Overdale in Telford.

During my time as a driver in this crazy industry, I have on rare occasions had to deal with 'troublesome' passengers, but to date, I have never had a moment's hassle with school students. I was taught very early in my career that behaviour breeds behaviour; it is very difficult to have a go at someone who is being nice and respectful towards you. I treated the students fairly, never giving them any undue hassle, and they were always happy (as they still are today) to see the bus roll up with me behind the wheel, giving no hassle and getting no hassle!

Of course, I've had a couple of incidents, but generally speaking I managed to get through the day. I remember the time when (at Select) I thought the students from Cheslyn Hay School were continually pressing the bell. This devilish practice can be most annoying; something had to be done, or so it appeared!

It is common practice for Ben Brown (Select Bus Services) to allocate whenever possible the same bus daily to a particular duty. One of the main reasons for this is the number of students travelling, if a school journey is part of any particular duty. So I was operating a school run on no.8 duty which included the Cheslyn Hay School. The bus I was allocated was a large 'Dennis Dart', with tartan moquette. On one afternoon run from the school back to Essington, the bell seemed to be ringing very frequently. I stopped the bus and called back to the students, 'Okay children, leave the bells alone, please.' They hated being referred to by that term. Almost as one voice, they replied that it wasn't them, and no-one was touching the bell buttons. And yet, the bells kept ringing!

Upon my return to the depot, I mentioned it to Dave Farrow, a (now former) driver colleague. He told me, 'Yes that bus does that sometimes Scriv.'

'Oh right, cheers Dave.'

The next time I had that particular bus (the former fleet no.1), the same thing happened. So I again brought the bus to a halt. Before I could speak, the students at the rear of the bus shouted: 'It's not us, Driver. We haven't touched the bells, honest.'

'No, I know you haven't, but listen to this.' I then launched into a very convincing tale about the bus being haunted by the ghost of an old man. I told them it was the last bus home, and it was pouring with rain. The old man struggled from his seat, to the front of the saloon, and told the driver that he'd wanted the previous stop. They were heading along a narrow country lane somewhere in deepest Scotland (tartan moquette). The driver said, in a curt and berating voice: 'Well you should have pressed the bell.' The old man insisted that he had, but the driver carried on regardless. The old man pleaded with the driver to stop, but it was a good quarter-mile before he did, shouting abuse at his elderly, confused and distressed passenger as he opened the doors. The old man struggled to alight before the nasty bus driver closed the doors and sped off! And as he attempted to make his slow journey back to his intended bus stop, the elderly gentleman suffered a fatal heart attack!

I went on to say that from that day to this, the bells spasmodically sound on this bus. And every time that particular driver drove the bus, he saw the old man in his rear-view mirror. Eventually, he and every single one of his colleagues refused to drive that bus... so the company had no alternative but to sell it cheaply.

I added that our boss had purchased the vehicle, but had been reluctant to tell us the ghost story, concerned that we would also refuse to drive it.

'Well, you're driving it now, mate,' someone observed.

'Yes,' I said, 'I don't mind driving it for triple pay. Only snag is, it's now started happening on other buses.'

That delightful yarn brought an end, at least for a time, to students pressing the bells for fun on all of our no.71 Cheslyn Hay School journeys.

Whenever anyone did give me any shit on other service routes, I reacted in kind. On one occasion, I almost passed a stop, not seeing the intending passenger as she was hidden away in the shelter until the last second, before jumping out and waving her arms. I stopped the bus and she strolled up to me as I opened the doors. She made the mistake of remaining on the pavement as she berated me: 'Are you sure you should be driving a bus? You nearly left me standing; is your eyesight ok?' I replied: 'Yes, it's fine thanks. I can see the sun, and that's about ninety-three million miles away.' And before she could reply, or board, I closed the doors and drove off!

Another incident came about when I was on the no.51 service from Arleston to Shawbirch via Wellington Bus Station. A lady boarded in Arleston, and gave me a quid for her fare. Upon counting out her change, I found I was a penny – yes, just a single penny – short. I explained the situation; most people would have said to just forget it. Not this one! She began to moan at me for the fact that I owed her a penny, and she wanted it before she got off at the end of her journey. The fact is, we didn't have to give change, it was a concession, but she wouldn't have it. Anyway, upon reaching Wellington, the passengers began alighting; most saying thank you, to which I responded likewise. When this lady arrived at my side, towering above me because the cab was very low in those Noddy buses, she demanded her penny, saying she wasn't getting off until she got it. I hadn't got a penny, and after her appalling attitude I wasn't going to give her a two-pence-piece, so we reached stalemate. The remaining passengers couldn't get past her, and so they too began moaning at me for not having sufficient change... what a nerve!

All of a sudden, a single penny was tossed over their heads, hitting the windscreen before coming to a rest on the dash. 'Here's your blasted penny, now piss off!'

Those (welcome) dulcet tones came from a very well-known Arleston lady who was renowned for speaking her mind, and taking the piss out of Jeremy Kenny at every opportunity! On this occasion, however, the matter was duly resolved!

Most of the 'old hands' at the depot welcomed us, but as with everything, or different situations, one or two of the so-called 'big bus drivers' refused to acknowledge us, which was fine by me. I have never been much of a mixer, preferring my own company. I can be the life and soul of the party when the mood takes me but by and large, I suppose I am, as Tina quite rightly says, more than a little anti-social. I was never the first to raise my hand whenever another bus came towards me; I did it once and was blanked... that was enough!

Some of the established drivers, however, were immediately sociable with us, including Kenny Rogers, Colin Turner, Dave Skitt, Mel Gough, John Hodges, Don Bates and Dave Richards (or 'DR' as he was referred to by many). Ken was known for sounding his horn at every opportunity; everyone knew, and liked, Ken. Dave Forsyth – and John Morgan – had been part of the team of instructors (which included, from other depots, John Perkins and Harry Pratt), who trained the Walsall drivers, so we had at least a couple of people we knew when we arrived, even if we couldn't exactly class them as friends yet.

One morning, I walked into the drivers' room to find a young lad, smartly attired in a light grey Midland Red tunic, complete with shirt and company tie. He was studying the duty rota for the following week. I thought how he must be the youngest busman I'd ever seen. Then without warning, he slammed both hands onto the counter and shouted, 'I don't believe it.' I asked what troubled him, and he said, 'I'm on fuckin' late duties again next week!' And then he stormed out. I was gobsmacked.

The lad, I was to discover later, was young Craig Collier (his father Rupert was to join the company in due course). Craig rode around with Kenny Rogers all day, so whatever duty Ken was doing, so was Craig! Everyone thought Craig would join the industry when he became of age to do so, but alas, he chose another path.

Another lad who did the same as Craig, but with a number of drivers, was Jeremy Kenny. He did join us, and is still in the industry. He has now clocked up twenty-five years with Midland Red and Arriva, and is currently working out of the Telford depot. These lads were a godsend to new drivers because, if asked, they would go with the driver until he or she was confident enough to go out alone on whichever route they were assigned to.

A funny story involving Jeremy: I had been transferred to Cannock depot as Passenger Services Manager (or Garage Manager) in May 2000. A while later, Jeremy and I got tickets for Manchester United's European cup-tie against the French outfit Lilles, at Old Trafford. It was an evening kick-off, and we made the journey in his car. Upon our arrival, we found a secure car park, where we left the car. Jeremy got a credit-card-sized ticket, and off we went. After the game, we arrived back at the car park to find the gates locked, and not a soul about! I said we shouldn't have had that pint after waiting to see the players leave the stadium, but it was what it was!

We decided that we would have to try and find some cheap digs for the night, after having visited a police station to ask for help, only to be told, 'Do one lads, we can't help you.' We trekked all around the city but there was no room in the inn... any inn! Well, United were at home; enough said.

'What the fuck we gonna do, mate?' I asked my young buddy.

'Dunno, we'll just have to keep trying to find somewhere.'

On we trekked. Eventually, we came across a scruffy-looking gaff that had obviously seen better days. It looked that bad from the outside that we actually contemplated kipping out in the open air... but we decided to give it a go. We were greeted by an aged bloke who looked like he'd just finished mining coal. We enquired as to whether he had a couple of vacant rooms for just the one night. He replied: 'I've only got the one room; you'll have to make do with that.'

Beggars can't be choosers, as they say, and we considered that it probably had twin beds... wrong!!!!

We were led up some creepy, dark stairs to a tiny room which quite obviously hadn't seen any form of decorative improvement since the place was built... with just one double bed, which was covered by a tatty, dishevelled quilt that would not have looked out of place in a dog basket! I looked at my mate with genuine concern. He turned to our host and said, in a resolute manner, 'Cheers.'

It cost us a massive forty pounds each for the privilege of listening to each other fart and snore all fuckin' night in that horrible place!

The following morning, we left without having breakfast; surprise, surprise. We were both glad to be back out in the fresh air, but we couldn't remember where we had left the car. So we wandered around looking for any familiar landmarks. On our way, we stumbled upon a burger van, so took advantage of an offer to cook us one each... for an arm and a leg! We should have both been at our respective depots by now, so I rang Cannock (and

Wellington), explaining our plight. Brian Campbell, my staff manager, just pissed himself! 'See you later then, Scriv,' he said between loud hoots of laughter.

Eventually, we found the car park, but the gates were still shut. As we looked around, scratching our heads in total disbelief, a gentleman arrived. Quickly, we approached him, asking what time the car park opened. He eyed us rather quizzically before producing a credit-card-sized ticket similar to the one Jeremy had been issued the day before, then explaining that the card had to be placed in the appropriate slot. The gates would open, and you could go in and fetch your car; pressing a button to close them again afterwards.

'Hang on mate,' I said, looking at my equally puzzled friend, 'so all we had to do was put our card in there, and we could have got our car out?'

'Er, yes; it's that simple.'

So because neither of us realised what the procedure was for retrieving Jeremy's car, we spent a very expensive night in Manchester, in a dingy B&B, in one bloody bed, fully dressed... and not daring to turn over!

We eventually arrived back at Cannock depot at about 1500hrs.

I settled quietly into my new flat; some of my colleagues at the depot very kindly helped me with bits of furniture, etc. One of the office girls, Sarita, who was at the time married to Dave Adshead, another of the more sociable drivers (lost to us now, as are many of the people who were at Wellington back then), very kindly offered to do my laundry. I still have the blue canvas bag which she used to fetch and return my washing in. Sarita was very kind to me, and I appreciated it. She is one of my 'social media friends' today, along with many of my colleagues from back in the day.

Very often, I would choose to walk to work. It took me about an hour, but it was mostly downhill. The strange thing is, I'd get picked up regularly by colleagues commuting from Dawley, Woodside and Brookside... but once I started walking back home, up the steep Dawley Road, I hardly ever got a lift! Looking on the bright side, it was good exercise, and I enjoyed it.

Sometime after moving to Wellington, Midland Red North came up with the strange (as it transpired) idea that it ought to have a depot in Oakengates. A number of drivers, including all of us ex-Walsall personnel, were told that we were moving to the new depot. Here's the rub: the new 'depot' consisted of a porta-cabin situated at the top end of Wellington Depot (indoors)! But all the buses ran out of Wellington, so we were another branch of MRN in name only... just like Walsall, I suppose. Needless to say, that little 'enterprise' never took off, either.

I suppose I must have made an acceptable impression on my new colleagues, because I was asked to stand as a union shop steward towards the end of the 1980s. I agreed to take part in the ballot, the result being a landslide victory for me. In fact, I was told that I had won the most votes ever cast (seventy-four) in a Wellington union ballot. It was a requirement that every employee, or at least the platform and engineering staff, join the T&GWU, so I considered that if I was a paid-up member, I should attend the union meetings. And I always spoke up on subjects that mattered to me. This was the reason, perhaps, why I was asked to stand.

In early October 1990, a ballot for the office of Garage Union Chair was to take place. I was set to stand against established shop steward Colin Turner, who by this time was a good friend. On 8th February 1990, however – one day before the ballot – I withdrew my interest, posting the following on the union notice board:

Dear Members
My reason for not standing against COLIN TURNER for the chair of Wellington Union Committee is that after a lot of thought, I decided that Colin was more suitable, and would be a bigger asset to the union, in the position of Chair (given his time with the company, and presence on the committee) than I would be.

Also, I considered that holding a ballot at the moment, would be detrimental to the "understanding" the committee now has.

Alan Scriven (shop steward)

I enjoyed my time on the union committee, but was destined to return to more familiar roles (i.e. management) in the fullness of time.

Wellington Depot had a very good sports and social club, which organised many attractive and entertaining functions. I was particularly partial to the inter-depot quizzes, which always guaranteed great fun. And the trips were just brilliant. We visited places like Gulliver's Kingdom, and even went abroad on two occasions: France and Belgium (although these trips may have occurred after the demise of the club).

In early 1992, the club hit the rocks! Below is the notice of confirmation which was posted in February:

Dear Members
With reference to the meeting held on 05/02/92.

Due to the lack of support from members over the last twelve months, your S&S Club has lost a considerable amount of money on functions, due to lack of interest. Therefore this has resulted in the resignation of some committee members.

Due to the lack of committee members, we have no alternative but to disband the S&S Club.

As from Friday 07/02/92 head office will be instructed to cancel all subscriptions from your wages, and a full bank statement will be put on the notice board.

Therefore there will be one final function, open to all members, at no charge, as the money is yours.

The date and venue is to be arranged.

(On behalf of the S&S Club Committee)

I was totally against this decision, and told the committee so, in an 'open letter', which was posted on the S&S club notice board:

Having read the notice, informing members of the committee's decision to disband, and close down the Club, I would like, as a member, to say the following:

Firstly, the decision to close down, without an extraordinary meeting being called, during which, the members would be invited to attend, and discuss the matter fully, is extremely unprofessional, and in contrast to recognised democratic committee procedure.

Furthermore, the committee cannot without a mandate in the constitution, disband the club, and then decide what happens to funds already paid in by the members.

I for one, and I believe the vast majority of other members do not wish to see the demise of the Sports and Social Club. I therefore urge the committee to reconsider its individual decisions to resign, and if agreement cannot be reached, then the existing members should be invited to form a new committee.

The club should not suffer for what seems to be 'personality clashes' amongst its committee.

I would also ask the Secretary or Treasurer to retract from its instruction to H.O. to cancel our subscriptions because this is too severe and extreme a measure before adult and responsible discussion has been given a fair opportunity.

In closing, may I offer my sincere thanks to all committee members for all their previous work and well meant efforts.
<u>*Alan Scriven*</u>

Oh dear! I was beginning to make a name for myself. Jim Churm, a much respected so-called 'big bus driver', and a member of the committee, objected strongly to my wording, but after a chat, we sorted things out amicably, I think, although things were never the same again between us.

During the 1990s, we enjoyed many days out, and indeed weekends to places as far-flung as Scotland. Colin Turner was at the organising forefront of the majority (if not all) of our trips.

We went to Scotland twice, actually; firstly to Kirkcaldy, to engage in a friendly football match against a fellow bus company team. My eldest son Marc, who would have been about sixteen years old at that time, joined me on the trip. Almost immediately after Colin Turner (who officiated during the game) blew his whistle to start the match, it became obvious that the Scots were going to run up a 'cricket score' unless he acted quickly, and so without a hint of bias (??) Colin sent off their best player after about ten minutes! His bold action, however, only served to increase the Scots' determination to stuff us, which they duly did!

This reminds me of the time I did exactly the same as Colin had done, whilst I was refereeing a game at the Longmynd Adventure Camp[2] I had to 'red card' a lad because his exceptional talent meant that the opposing team(s) had no chance! And as the inter-tent football tournament was part of the overall competition for the best group (tent) I had to ensure the result was... well... not rigged... but... er...

When I stopped the play and called the lad over, I said that I

---

[2]The Longmynd Adventure Camp is a children's charity which I was part of as a beneficiary and later, voluntary staff member (rising through the 'ranks' to become its leader - under the title of 'Skipper' - in 1990) from 1965 to 1998 inclusive. I have written the early history -1958 to 1998 - of the charity in the three books mentioned previously.

had no alternative but to show him the red card. A very bewildered young lad then quite rightly demanded an explanation as to how (his words) I had arrived at this ridiculous decision. So both teams waited with baited breath, as did the two very confused 'assistant referees'. I put my hand on the lad's shoulder (because one could back then) and said: 'I'm sorry son; I'm sending you off for playing the ball.' The whole place erupted in raucous laughter; even the 'victim'. They all thought I was joking. I wasn't. The George Best impersonator had to go! As a way of apology, however, I told him he could keep the ball after serving a three-match suspension! I know; terrible. But it was all with the best (no pun intended) intentions... and the lad took it in his stride, because he could still show his impressive skills in our regular 'Staff versus Kids' football matches. We had to keep the tent groups pretty equal on points (until the final few days), as the awarding and deducting of points – which created competition – was our only form of discipline.

On a trip to Edinburgh, we stopped at Abingdon services. I was one of the last to disembark, before casually walking into the building where most of my mates were already seated. To my utter amazement, I was stopped at the entrance by two uniformed police officers. One asked me for my name. I told him, and he said, 'Come with us please, sir.'

They led me into the services area, where all my colleagues were sat, eyeing me in what I soon discovered was fake concern, and disbelief. Then the second officer said, 'Alan Scriven, I should arrest you for displaying the English flag in the rear window of a coach you are travelling on, in our country.'

I looked at them both, then at everyone in the room; I was in severe shock, I'm sure. I looked back at the cops and said, 'I don't understand.'

They kept their faces straight until one of the McLafferty brothers called out: 'Brilliant, mate; thanks very much.' Then the two cops pissed themselves laughing, as did everyone in the room! I felt acute embarrassment very briefly, before aiming a volley of insults at my Scottish colleagues.

After the match, or should I say the 'mauling' in Kirkcaldy, we joined our hosts for an evening of fun and entertainment. But during the evening, I noticed one of the Scots lads eying me as he made his way around the room, stopping at every table, except ours! I said to Marc, 'That geezer with the padded jacket on is looking for trouble, I'm sure. He keeps looking over here. I can't remember fouling him during the game.' 'Oh take no notice, Dad, it'll be okay mate,' Marc answered with more than an air of apparent disinterest.

Later in the evening, that same suspicious-looking guy got up and announced to everyone: 'The English guy over there,' pointing straight at me, 'does a lot of voluntary charity work for poor kids, like I was.' He had everyone's attention as he continued: 'And when I was a kid, if it hadn't been for people like him, we would have had nothing, and never would have had a holiday.' I looked at Marc, and he just nodded his head. He knew this was coming. 'So thank you all for your kind donation to the kids' charity this guy works hard for, voluntarily.' He called me to him, and gave me a bag of cash as he shook my hand. 'Well done mate,' was all he said before making his way back to his table. I said a few words of gratitude, to a beautiful round of applause. And the money, which I asked Colin Turner to count with me later, was duly paid to our charity's treasurer, on my return home.

Marc told me later that a couple of our lads had mentioned my charity work and our Scottish friend had got wind of it, maybe through the McLaffertys, and decided to act. What a wonderfully kind gesture from a complete stranger!

The Scots came south of the border for a game we played near to Cannock depot, and again they beat us convincingly; great times, though, enjoyed by everyone, including some mates I still have today: Colin Turner, Dave Wilde, Simon Gray-Davis, and Dennis and Charlie McLafferty.

When we visited Edinburgh, it was a chilly day, with dark clouds full of impending rain. Edinburgh's impressive castle is famous for firing one of its cannon at precisely 1300hrs, every day... apparently. On this particular day, however, Marc and I were walking along Princes Street with a fellow driver, and friend, Nick McDowell, waiting for the cannon to blast. As the clock struck 1300hrs – nothing! 'What's happened to the cannon?' I said with a quizzical look. And quick as a flash, Nick retorted: 'I bet the caps are damp, Scriv!' We roared with laughter... just as the cannon roared its response!

We had some great times at wonderful Wellington. I remember being on service no.53, which operated between the Brookside estate in South Telford, and The Humbers at Donnington in the north, via Oakengates and Telford town centre. It was a beautiful summer day. I arrived at The Garrison bus shelters, just prior to the service destination point, to find David Law (alias 'Digger') sitting in a deck chair, legs outstretched, with his shirt unbuttoned to the waist; trousers rolled up; sunglasses on, and a cold drink in his hand! His bus, the no.52 service to the Bell Gate pub terminus, which should have been ten or fifteen minutes in front of my 53, was parked up enjoying the unofficial break, too. I asked him if the bus had broken down. He replied: 'No mate, it's fine.' 'What are you doing then, Dave?' I asked. He replied, as he lifted his sunglasses to his forehead, 'What's it look like, Scriv? I'm having five; fuck it, mate.' Fair enough. I continued on to my destination. Later that day, I asked Dave if he had completed his journey to the Bell Gate before resuming service back to Telford. His reply was typical: 'What do you think, Scriv.' It wasn't a question! Dave is the son of Winston Law, who was one of the senior drivers at Wellington for a number of years.

By and large, we all did what was expected of us out on the

road, but if we could get away with pulling the odd flanker, we did. That's one of the reasons why I think the best bosses are the ones that have actually done their time as a driver. I'm not saying they (or I, when I became a manager) turned a blind eye; far from it – I mean you couldn't 'pull the wool', but having been a driver, one could perhaps ascertain without too much difficulty whether further action might be necessary regarding complaints. Some people complained about drivers for a hobby, I'm sure.

Passengers of a certain age are given a free bus pass by their respective councils and whichever council the pass is supplied by determines the conditions of use. Most stipulate that the senior citizen pass could not be used before 0930hrs (and during my early career there was also a limit to using it in the afternoon too, between 1530 and 1800hrs if memory serves –but I might be wrong here – which was ended a good few years ago). Some of these pass holders, however, insisted on being at the bus stop well before 0930hrs. Drivers would stop their bus because usually there were other intending passengers who would be paying a fare or be in possession of a pass (usually a 'five-rider' or a 'multi-rider'). The senior citizen, however, would chance her/his arm by holding out their pass and saying, 'Am I too early?' Knowing full well that they were! This almost daily-heard phrase earned them the nickname of 'the Twirlies'.

Some elderly passengers would be given a bag of National Bus Tokens of various cash denominations, which would be issued as I believe an alternative to passes. If these were presented for a fare, drivers would be instructed to give change (if they had it), as if real money had been paid. This sometimes riled a few drivers, but at the end of the day it wasn't their money! And some of the punters would offer drivers a large number of tokens for a little less actual cash than the token total; this act would pay for a cup of tea and a sandwich for the driver at break time. I never saw any harm in that because all sides were on a winner.

Speaking of cash and tokens, Keith Danks, a Wellington driver during my time at that wonderful depot, used to have a saying at the end of his duty: 'Well that's me, weighed in, paid in, booked off and fucked off.'

Keith had a small aeroplane which he used – he said – for (amongst other things) delivering mail for the Post Office, and if he knew any of us were flying somewhere on holiday, he would always tell us that that wasn't real flying; then offer to take us with him on a delivery. As far as I know, no-one accepted!

Chapter Three

"Wacky Races"

'On public transport you see things that no-one should have ever to see.' (Anonymous)

Towards the end of the 1980s – 10th March 1989, to be exact – I passed my Class 1 PCV driving test. I wasn't tied to Midland Red by another indemnity, because I took the test privately. I had realised that public transport was where my employment future lay, so decided to get the best licence possible, in order to hopefully achieve more success. The company had begun putting drivers through the class 1 training course, and I was very grateful to be invited. But I failed the test first time, after an incident in Shrewsbury. That incident, however, turned out to be a blessing, because rather than take the test again with Midland Red, I considered that it should be my own affair. I passed at my first attempt with a private tutor.

I didn't have to wait long before Martin Bufton took full advantage of my 'step up', as he called it. He began giving me (and others who had also passed) the occasional duty from the 'big bus' rota. The management's intention was to get rid of this rota (and therefore the higher rate) so that as the older, longer-serving drivers either retired or passed on, so the rota decreased in number. The big bus drivers weren't all happy about this, but it happened anyway. And drivers like me were delighted to be given a chance to drive the larger buses. Some even enjoyed getting behind the wheel of Leyland Tigers, or Dominants, as they were also known. I hated these buses, to be honest, as much as I did the coaches. The Leyland Nationals were my favourite; semi-automatic, single saloon buses, which were so easy and nice to drive, in my opinion.

We were issued with new contracts on 01/01/1990 as a result of our increased capability. The contract stated that we were now employed as Mini Bus, Midi Bus, and Big Bus drivers (just a case of the company covering all bases). Cool... but as I said above, the company wanted to do away with the big bus rate, so there was no increase in pay for us. My payslip dated 28/12/90 shows that for fifty-three hours worked during the previous week, I earned £159:69 net. Rumour had it that cleaners like Kathy Smith were being paid more than us!

The garage manager at this point in my career was Ray Griffiths, assisted by Neale Wallace. Both men were decent enough to work for, but I didn't completely trust Neale. When I joined Midland Red, Neale held the position of Sales Manager. His grin reminded me of a lady called Joan, who had a bread and cake shop in Hawksford Crescent, Low Hill (when I was a boy) which was always full of customers; she had that same permanent grin, but you crossed her at your peril!

Our depot operated, amongst many other services, the no.2 and no.12 routes, which served south Telford in an anti-clockwise and clockwise route, respectively. From Monday 2nd September 1991, however, Shearings Coach and Bus Co. began operating both services, in direct opposition to Midland Red. So began the ever memorable 'Wacky Races' – brilliant fun, if one didn't take it too seriously; some did, unfortunately.

Ray and Neale sought to try and cancel out the Shearings 'threat' by organising a rota made up of – in their words – 'the best drivers' to ensure the company's success in driving (no pun intended) the opposition off 'our' routes.

Most of the drivers applied for this special rota, me being one of them. The bosses then considered all applications, and in due course posted a list of the chosen few. I was not on the initial list, but I did make first reserve. The unsuccessful drivers then became unhappy about their non-selection, and began taking the piss out of the successful ones, with jibes along the lines of: 'Best drivers, my arse!'; 'How the hell did he get on it?'; 'She couldn't drive a pig to fuckin' market!'; 'Better not ask me to go on 'em now,' and so on.

Before the retaliation against Shearings began in earnest, one of our drivers dropped out, and I was asked if I was still interested in joining the 2/12 rota. I immediately reaffirmed my interest, and was told by Ray that I was joining a team of 'ace drivers' who had been chosen to perform a difficult task. A meeting was called in the conference room at the depot. The gaffers explained in fine detail what the main purpose was: to cancel out Shearings. We were given carte-blanche (within reason) to do what we felt was necessary to succeed, but the bottom line was: we were MRN (Midland Red North) bus drivers and therefore expected to drive safely and professionally at all times, with passenger safety and comfort at the forefront of our responsibilities. Well, we did drive to the expected standard, on most occasions. To be fair, so too did the opposition.

The unofficial protagonists of our team were Dave Richards* and Colin Turner. These guys were the hub of our operations during the Wacky era. Their opposite numbers, Les Whitehouse and (the now late) Pete Simpson, proved almost equal to the task in hand (sorry, Les).

Dave and Colin were staunch union men, and worked alongside our liaison officer, Richie Benting; a rather quick-tempered guy, who knew his union responsibilities and performed them well. Richie is another ex-colleague now lost to us.

The so-called 'cream of the depot' 2/12 rota didn't last long, due to the nature of the industry. There was regularly an occasion when Martin had to ask someone to work on the Wackies and whenever he did, hardly anyone refused. Well, I suppose it was a bit of kudos to be asked, in spite of their previous feelings!

You had to know what you were doing on the Wackies, and to keep your wits about you at all times, and I – like most others – slipped up now and then. On one occasion, Les Whitehouse was driving the bus in front of me, and arrived in the bus station with a seated load (bus full), according to Dave Richards. I trailed in a few minutes behind him with about five passengers. 'DR' (as he came to be known at Wellington) went ballistic! 'How the fuck did you let him get in front of you and come in with his bus full to the gunnels, Scriv?' 'I didn't know where the fucker was,' I replied. DR then threatened to have me off the Wackies, if it happened again. Normally, a threat of this nature would be enough for me to lose my rag and say 'stick it', but I decided against it on this occasion.

Drivers depended on a signal from one's colleagues approaching from the opposite direction for clues as to how far the Shearings (or Timeline, as they later became known) driver was in front of your bus. Don Housden would give you an almost hidden signal, using his fingers to indicate approximately how many minutes in front of you the opposition was; almost as if he thought there were spies standing on your platform!

Most of us drivers (on both sides) stitched each other up with a smile on our faces, but that said, there were the occasional bust-ups. I remember running Dennis Patterson ragged one afternoon on the no.12 route, and he let it get to him. I pulled into the bus station and went inside to use the toilet. As I came out, Dennis slammed me up against the wall and threatened to inflict all sorts of damage upon my person if I did it to him again. Dennis was a giant of a man, but I defended myself, as I always did, and we became friends again soon after. It was unfair to react the way Dennis had because we were all doing what was best for our respective companies.

A nice quality Dennis possessed (as an inspector) was the fact that if he was called upon to do a bit of driving in service, he would always give you the 'thumbs down' signal if he was coming towards you, and had passed (or even encountered) an inspector colleague. The signal is an age-old practice to warn your colleagues approaching from the opposite direction that an inspector was waiting for them ahead. The 'heads up' offered an opportunity for the driver to make sure everything was in order, i.e. being on time, and correct use of the ticket machine. There are a multitude of reasons for running a little bit late, but there is not one single reason or excuse for operating earlier than the timetable states.

Dennis had joined Shearings/Timeline after leaving Midland Red. He had served as an inspector as well as a driver during his time with the Red, as it was affectionately called by most. 'Most' did not include Graham Martin, however, who owned another (small) company called Green Bus Service. No, Graham referred to the company as 'Midland Shed', or 'Midland Dead', much to the amusement of anyone who wasn't part of the Red, i.e. my current gaffer Ben Brown, who worked for Graham after a short stint at Midland Shed, Cannock.

Drivers committed as many 'dirty tricks' against the opposition as they could get away with. One, performed by both sets of drivers was, when on service 2, you would wait at the first stop on the Woodside estate, until the opposition vehicle came into view from behind, at the top of Majestic Way (which runs between Little Dawley and the roundabout just before the Woodside turn). As soon as you caught site of the bus, you would slowly pull away, mopping up the waiting passengers on the estate as you did so. But the chasing (crafty) driver might skip Woodside, assuming that it would be pointless and fruitless to follow the bus in front so closely, and instead bypass it, heading straight into Madeley, as long as they had no passengers wishing to alight on Woodside. They would then sit in Madeley for five minutes or so before gently pulling away and heading for Brookside with all passengers from Madeley on their bus: great fun and games!

Actually, how you worked it depended on the time of day. During the mornings, one would concentrate on staying out as long as possible, in order to bring the maximum number of passengers into town. Then, once the sun had tripped over the yardarm, it was a case of getting round the route and back into the bus station as soon as possible, to board as many homeward-bound passengers as you could before being given the word to depart, usually by DR. As I recall, the most regular drivers on the Wacky rota for MRN were, in no particular order: John Edge, Debbie Ashford, her dad Peter, Dennis Williams, Dave Adshead, Winston Law, Mick 'Buster' Edwards, Ian Stevens, Don Housden, Kenny Rogers, Mick Teece, John Salter, Bill Parton, Mick Simmonds, Colin Turner, DR and me. My apologies if I have forgotten anyone.

For Shearings, regulars included Les and Pete (as mentioned previously), Gerald Cooper, Tony York, John Hind, Max Jasper, Alicia Wakeford, Derek Maddy, Charlie and Calvin Hayward, Jim Green, Brian Stokes, Pat O'Hanlon, John Smith, Terry Capell and big Dennis P.

John Smith joined us at Wellington when MRN took over Timeline, and we became friends, as we still are. Currently, John works with me at Select, after a spell at Arriva, Shrewsbury. Alicia became Mrs Wakeford following her marriage to Norman, a colleague of mine at the Red, who worked out of our Bridgnorth outstation.

Just looking at those names above, it saddens me to say that at least a dozen of those drivers have now passed away. God bless them all.

It was whilst working on the Wackies that I met my second wife, Nicki. I noticed her whilst working on the minibuses, travelling between Brookside and the Town Centre. I took a liking to her immediately, but took it no further until one day, straight out of the blue, I drove a Leyland National onto our no.12 stand (all the stands were pre-determined) at Telford bus station, secured it, and left it to board the no.52 that Nicki was sat on, awaiting its departure. I walked straight up to her and told her I wanted her on my bus! Very bold, you might think. She refused, however, saying that the no.52 went out before the no.12, so she would remain where she was, thank you. Ah well, you win some...

Eventually, I reversed off the stand and set off on my merry way around south Telford, trying to stay just a few stops in front of the opposition. Upon my arrival back at the bus station, DR boarded my bus and gave me a note from 'that blonde girl you fancy from Brookside'. The note from Nicki was an invitation to go out with her one evening. She included her number in the brief message, and I rang her that evening. We arranged a date... I picked her up, and we spent a nice evening together before I took her home – her home!

From then on, things moved much faster than they should have really, and we were married in Wellington on 11th September 1993, just six months after meeting. As I say in one of my previous books, we all have degrees in hindsight! Having said that, I enjoyed every day I spent with Nicki.

The marriage lasted less than two years. The problem I had when everything went south with my marriage was that after we wed, I put my flat out to rent and moved into Nicki's small bungalow. Therefore, when it all went tits up, by which time we were living in a council house on Brookside, I was effectively homeless, at least until the tenancy agreement on my flat in Dawley expired. I suppose I could have insisted on the agents evicting my tenant, but making her homeless was not, I decided, an option. Fortunately, however, my now late sister Pat and her now late husband Les very kindly put me up. But not any old 'put me up'. Oh no – they gave me my own room and even had Sky TV installed for me! Our brother Billy had been living at Pat's since the death of our mother, but he had the attic, so it wasn't as if I was pushing his nose out, so to speak. My moving in didn't go down very well with Pat's eldest daughter, however... well, she was best friends with my younger sister, to whom I hadn't spoken since Mom's passing (and we still don't speak – no worries, though, that's fine by me).

It was both Nicki's and my second marriage. I haven't married again since, but I know she did. I have no idea what her marital status is today, but I wish her well.

I digress. As I said above, we stitched each other up around the routes, with a smile on our faces – in the main. But sometimes, situations out on the road came to a boiling point at the bus station, e.g. Dennis Patterson and me. Also, Winston Law and Les Whitehouse never saw eye-to-eye on the Wackies. On another occasion when things came to a head, Colin Turner got involved in a slanging match with a member of the opposition's team; his name was Jim Green. Jim and I got on well, but on the day in question he and Colin let a heated argument drift into a challenge. The result being that the two of them walked side by side across the road and out of sight of prying eyes, to 'sort it out one way or another', in Colin's words. I don't know what happened over the road but they both returned none the worse for wear, thankfully, and soon were 'friends' again. Another story involving Colin Turner whilst on Wackies was the time our manager Ray Griffiths asked him to collect a tax disc from Head Office. Ray told him to make the journey in his bus. What Colin didn't know was that the opposition had instructed one of their drivers, namely Pete Rogers, to 'follow Turner wherever he goes'. Colin set off for Cannock in true and obedient fashion, and Pete did likewise. The first time Colin realised he was being followed was when it finally dawned on poor Pete that Colin was not trying to lose him on yet another Wacky circuit! Colin clocked him trying to turn around on the A5! And apparently, when both were back in Telford bus station, Pete told Colin that after turning his bus around, he then got himself lost! There was lots of good fun and sport between the drivers... well, most of us.

I can't remember when the so called "Wacky Races" actually finished. But the end (proper) came when MRN took over Shearings, which had by then become Timeline, but I'm not exactly sure when that was. MRN became known as Arriva (which I was told means nothing in any language); it was so called, apparently, to attract more female passengers to use the bus towards the end of the 1990s. I had no problem with that!

The good thing is that after the passing of all the intervening years, those of us fortunate to still be around are all friends, by and large, and in touch again, if only on social media. And we meet up to attend the occasional funeral of former colleagues in the industry. They are sad days, obviously, but those of us left reminisce about those long-gone times when we were all together, and thinking we would be forever; alas.

When the fun and games ended, I wrote a light-hearted poem to Les Whitehouse (specifically), and all the Shearings/Timeline drivers after the take-over:

An Ode to the Dude on the 12's and the 2's
Well Les, It's time to say goodbye
But it's all been a lot of fun.
You've tried to run us ragged,
And we've had you 'on the run'.
Scotty likes to run ten minutes down,
You Les, sometimes twenty,
But most of the time you got it right,
Because your passengers were plenty!
But all the good work you lads have done,
I'm really sorry to say
Is down the pan now Leslie boy,
Shearings have had their day.
It's breathed its last – it's over lads,
But no tears shall any of us shed.
And perhaps you'll now acknowledge Les,
That the cream is MIDLAND RED!

Happily, Les and everyone else accepted it in the spirit of friendship.

In the autumn of 1995, I passed the first of many courses in this crazy industry: Disability Awareness. In the same year, as a charity project, the Wacky drivers and others 'pulled' a minibus around the entire no.2 route. I use the word pulled lightly; we had to have the engine running in order for Hazel Skitt to steer the thing! But it was a great day, and we raised a good amount of cash. On another occasion, in 1996, we did the same again (but with a double-decker) on Safeways car park at Market Drayton; this time for our (now late) colleague Roy Cole's Cystic Fibrosis charity. Roy went on to be awarded the MBE for his tireless charity work for CF, of which he himself was a long-time sufferer. An extremely likeable chap was Roy, and always up for a laugh. God bless him. His award featured in the March 2002 edition of *ARRIVA NOW!* This monthly editorial had replaced the *BUSiness* magazine[3].

When the depot in Wellington was demolished, Martin Anderson (alias 'the Plug' to his friends) approached the council to inquire if any of the new streets could be named in Roy's memory (in honour of his many years of charity work whilst employed at the depot), and indeed, the depot itself. As a result, we now have Cole Terrace, Midland Mews, and Tellus Row. Nice one, Plug. Martin is a grandson of Dennis Patterson (mentioned previously), and is currently a colleague of mine at Select Bus Services.

Dave Richards became a good friend (as did Colin Turner) and when I left the depot to go to Cannock in 2000, we agreed that we would keep in touch. We made a promise to each other that we would have a telephone conversation every Christmas Day.

---

[3]It also reported that a colleague of ours from Wellington depot, Dave Porter, and his lovely wife Moira had received a blessing from His Holiness Pope John Paul II. A nice picture of Dave and Moira, with the blessing scroll, accompanied the article.

It pleases me to say that that promise has never faltered once! December 25th was decided so that neither of us would forget, as one might, if a random date was chosen. And during our telephone chat last Christmas (2022), we agreed to make our calls more regular.

Chapter Four

First Steps on the unsafe Arriva Ladder

In late January of 1996, a letter to the editor appeared in the *Shropshire Star* evening newspaper. It was written by a member of the public by the name of 'Mr Barker'. His intention obviously was to attempt to paint bus drivers as the 'rogues of the road'. I felt I had to respond, and as a result the following was published on 07/02/1996:

Having read Mr Barker's letter, in which he expresses his frank opinion of bus drivers, I considered that a reply from a bus driver was necessary in keeping with fairness.

In everything there will always be a difference of abilities, so maybe there are one or two bad bus drivers – I don't know of any however – but in the main, bus drivers, and in particular we in Telford, are extremely professional and go about our work with safety to our passengers; other road users, the public at large, and indeed our vehicles at the forefront of our responsibilities. It seems quite obvious that Mr Barker has very limited experience – if any – of driving anything larger than the average family car.

May I explain to him that there is, on occasions, and depending on the position of the bus-stop, or bus lay-by (assuming the bus can actually get into the lay-by as they are quite often full of parked cars) some difficulty for the bus driver to move off correctly, at the first attempt.

Invariably, the bus driver is forced to move the bus a short distance in order to afford a better and clearer view of what is going on behind, before committing to pulling away.

On many occasions buses, particularly the larger ones, have pulled out safely, only to have cars come upon them very suddenly at speeds far in excess of safety. And the snail-like pace of big buses trying to move away, and "clashing" with speeding motorists approaching from the rear, does at times cause what is now termed as 'road rage'.......very often on the part of the car / van driver!

I think my point is justified by Mr Barker's own words, when he 'speaks' of almost crashing into oncoming vehicles when overtaking parked up buses!

As for "always switching lanes on the one-way system in the town centre", Mr Barker should try and realise that buses have no alternative but to switch lanes, if they are ever going to get out of the bus station and proceed to their various destinations.

Also, I have yet to see a bus in the wrong lane at Hollinswood roundabout, but regularly witness car drivers who haven't got a clue how to approach this and other roundabouts, on a daily basis. Then they have the nerve to sound their horns in anger at the bus drivers who are wholly in the right!

May I close by respectfully inviting Mr Barker (or anyone else with his naive attitude) to spend a day with a bus driver, on a large bus, where he/she (they) will have an opportunity to witness themselves the constant hassle that the bus driver has to contend with day in, day out.

As if to substantiate everything I had said in that letter (at about the same time as it was published), I received a letter from Dave Forsyth (Training/Driving Standards Manager) confirming that due to my 'high standard of driving' I had earned the maximum bonus of £180 for a complete year's driving free from blameworthy accidents. And to follow this up, I became the first person at Telford Depot to pass the NVQ Level 2 (in Bus and Coach Driving and Customer Care), on 6th June 1996.

I think it very apt to say at this point (bearing in mind Mr

Barker's views above) that in my opinion the majority of road users, with the exception of bus, coach and truck drivers, and the emergency services, have no concept of what skills are required to drive a larger vehicle on Britain's roads on a daily basis! The average car driver is as dim as a Toc H lamp when it comes to 'reading' the road, and situations which arise when they meet a vehicle bigger than the one they're driving. I don't mean to be rude; it's simply a fact!

By this time in my career, Ray Faulkner was Traffic Manager, working under Peter Ralphs, who had come from Shrewsbury. Previous to Peter and Ray's term at Wellington, we had the pleasure of John Morrow's style of management, which wasn't bad, to be fair. Peter, if memory serves me well, was destined to return to Shrewsbury, as a result of 'rising star' Nick Newcombe coming to Wellington as General Manager, also from Shrewsbury. The company did like to move their managers around as and when it suited (as in my own case) senior management. Shrewsbury Depot was known as the managers' graveyard, which always baffled me... until I experienced first-hand the reason for this description, further down the line of my career in this crazy industry.

One day following a late duty (during Morrow's tenure at wonderful Wellington), I arrived for work at around mid-day, and went into 'despatch' to pick up my running board, cash bag, etc. Morrow appeared on the other side of the 'hatch' and said he wanted to see me. I collected my duty board from Martin Bufton and began to walk up the depot towards the office door. John came out, as I got there, asking: 'Did you pay your money in last night, Scriv?'

'Yes, John,' I replied, even naming the driver who was paying his money in at the same time as me. Drivers had a canvas cash bag which the day's takings were put into, and which at the end of duty would be dropped into the safe via a small pull-down door of sorts.

'It wasn't put into the safe,' Morrow said, with an obvious accusing look on his face.

'It was, John,' I insisted, looking him straight in the eye.

'I want to check your locker.' He wasn't giving up, or believing me.

We both walked back through the depot towards the drivers' room, not speaking at all. The office had a master key to all the lockers, so I was pretty certain mine (no. 4) had been checked already. I asked the question before opening it, and Morrow said no-one had been anywhere near it. Oh okay, then.

I opened my locker to reveal... nothing, except the cuddly toy Debbie Ashford had secretly put in there. Morrow straightened himself up, having bent to peer into my bottom-row locker, and said: 'I'm going to have to suspend you pending an investigation into the missing money.'

I hit back immediately: 'Can you open the safe first? I want to have a look inside it.'

'There's no need, it's already been checked.'

'Look, John, I paid my cash in last night, whatever you think, which by the way, you've made blatantly obvious. And you've made me open my locker in front of two other drivers, so do the decent thing and return the favour [emphasising this word]. Open the safe, John.'

'Okay, if you insist,' he grumbled. Morrow walked in front of me to the office door, and came out with the safe keys. He opened it with a critical look in his eye. All sorts of stuff was going through my head, i.e. where was my cash bag now?; who had taken it, and when? Drivers had no alternative but to trust the cash counters (not that we didn't), but I knew I had paid my money in on the previous night. My heart was in my mouth as Morrow slowly turned the key. And as the door swung open... there was my cash bag, tied up and obviously untouched by Dave Thomas and George Bruck; it was their job to count every driver's money and report any discrepancies. They had both somehow missed my bag when they emptied the safe, so were duty-bound to report my cash bag as 'missing'.

Morrow took the bag out, opened it and asked if he could check it. The company operated a 'shorts and overs' policy, so drivers did their best to ensure their takings were correct; and I was no exception. But Morrow obviously didn't believe me when I said I had paid in, so following his check, I did likewise, checking everything in that bag in front of him to show, hopefully, that I didn't trust him, either!

'I take it I can continue with getting myself sorted for today's duty?' I said, with more than a hint of sarcasm.

'Yes mate,' he grudgingly spluttered. No apology, though...

It actually hurts me a little to write like this about John Morrow, when I consider what a good working relationship we had enjoyed previously.

As I said earlier, Peter Ralphs took Morrow's place after he was called back to the hallowed grounds of Head Office, whereupon he was (later) 'anointed' as Area Manager West. Peter was a complex sort of guy, who seemed quiet and unassuming, but I got on really well with him; we became good friends. He came across as a well-educated man, who (seemingly) wasn't short of a bob or two. He took Mick Teece, Ian Tully and me to the Motor Show in Birmingham once, and he even joined us on a trip to Dublin which Ian Tully organised.

By this time, the depot (no. 24) was being referred to as 'Telford' as opposed to its rightful title of 'Wellington', which it had been for over sixty years.

Peter advertised (internally) for a small number of driver-clerks. The successful applicants would be placed on a special 'D.C. Rota', which included time on the road, and in the office. I fancied it, so I applied, quitting my role as a union shop steward beforehand.

One of my fellow applicants was a young lad called Ian Tully (to whom I have dedicated a chapter of this book). After we were both accepted, along with a few others, including Teresa

Bridgen (formerly Ellis), and Wilbur Bruck, we became very good friends. Ian's family had come over from Belfast during the 1980s to escape 'the Troubles'; his dad Billy was also a bus driver at Wellington, and a pretty good footballer, too; hailing from the same estate as the best footballer that I ever saw play the beautiful game – George Best.

Over the following years, up to the end of the decade/century/millennium, Ian (whom I had given the nickname 'Tul', by which he is still known to everyone) and I enjoyed a couple more promotions, and a few excursions out of the country. He called our outings 'Tul's Epic Journey No.1'... then 2, 3, 4, and so on.

I enjoyed working as a driver-clerk, as I know Tul did, too. And the extra money (Peter put our wages up to £12k per annum) came in very handy, as I had taken advantage of the council's offer to sell me my flat in Dawley.

Peter became a friend to Tul as well as to me, and another driver/engineer Mick Teece joined our little group. One morning, Peter invited me out to breakfast at the Little Chef on the A5 at Ivetsey Bank (the premises are host to Cafe India these days). We both enjoyed a Full English as he explained his intention to further promote Tul and me. He said he liked the way we worked and considered we could be more of an asset to the depot and therefore the company.

I couldn't see how he could do this, because he had a serving traffic manager in situ. Bob Purcell had been in his position for a good while. Everyone liked him, and no wonder; Bob was a good man who knew his job.

Mick Teece, alias 'Teecey' (or TC) joined me and Peter on our next breakfast outing. He had cornflakes and poured warm water over them, which amazed Peter, but not me. When I was a child, if we had cornflakes for breakfast (or maybe Weetabix) occasionally, we had warm water with it, not milk; Mom couldn't afford to give five of us milk, so warm water compensated.

We took it in turns to pay for our breakfast trips.

Peter Ralphs had his way; on 22nd April 1997, a Staff Vacancy notice appeared on the board. It stated that two vacancies existed at MRN Telford Depot for the position of Duty Manager.

Tul and I were told to apply, and as a result, on 21st April 1997 the following notice was posted:

STAFF APPOINTMENTS
Duty Managers
As part of the office reorganisation, which has been ongoing for some months, Alan Scriven and Ian Tully will be appointed Duty Managers at Telford Garage with effect from Monday 28 April 1997.

These new positions will give greater flexibility to the organisation and the office will now be manned between 0530 and 1900 to ensure that any problems with both staff and the public can be dealt with in a more satisfactory manner.

Martin Bufton will continue in his present position as Duty Supervisor and will be responsible for work coverage.

These new appointments will strengthen the local management team and ensure that the garage is well placed to take advantage of opportunities that may arise in the future.

Bob was effectively 'out in the cold'. He returned to his role as a driver, and although he never actually said anything (to me at least), I'm sure he resented us, for what Peter had done. It was a shame, because we had all been friends.

When Peter became a committee member of the Longmynd Adventure Camp children's charity I had been a part of since the mid-1960s, he brought Bob to one of our 'First Night' parties. Coincidentally, Bob's sister Jean Humphries was part of the Wolverhampton WRVS team, which selected some of the children who came to the Camp, in South Shropshire. Sadly, Jean was to pass away long before her time. I attended her funeral in my capacity as leader of the LAC.

56

The *BUSiness* magazine reported our promotion in its June 1997 edition, under the heading 'Cabinet Reshuffle'. It also announced the departure of office clerk Pat Cooper, who left the company after serving sixteen years at Wellington. When we had tea and toast in the office during the mid-morning, Pat watched us like a hawk; and woe betide anyone who tried to sneak an extra piece of toast!

Chapter Five

Ian George Tully

During our time together at Wellington, Tul and I took responsibility for the drivers and the rota, etc. This included hiring and firing. Tul will always say that he hired and I fired, but it wasn't always that way... I hired as well!

Accepting the more difficult task of the two responsibilities didn't affect me in any adverse manner; I just did my job and got on with it. If I was conducting a formal disciplinary hearing, I behaved very professionally, and never made the final decision regarding the outcome of such without adjourning to consider all of the facts. Of course, to some drivers I was the curse of the depot, and that continued at Cannock and Shrewsbury when I was Passenger Services Manager at both depots respectively. In fact, Tul told me very recently that he considered me a bit 'bolshy' when we worked together. This mildly degrading assessment, from a valued friend, came as somewhat of a surprise – even a shock – to me, as I had on no occasion thought that of myself. I tried to make him see that in order to do a successful job of the more difficult aspects of the position required, on occasions, a little more... aloofness, shall we say? Added to this, I have a tendency to be more of a natural 'loner' type (when not with a small number of trusted friends), which I accept comes across as negative in the personality stakes. Whereas Tul was usually upbeat and full of the joys, and liked by everyone, invariably, I wasn't.

The title 'Passenger Services Manager' came about when senior management decided on a 'change'. In effect, the PSM was the new title for Depot (or Garage) Manager. In my eyes, it was just a move to keep the pay rate down.

On our trips to Amsterdam, and actually everywhere else we went, Tul was a late riser; this used to vex me because I'm a morning person, so I rose early, never missed breakfast, and got on with the day.

One morning, after a night on the whisky, he absolutely refused to leave his bed. Instead, we arranged to meet at 1300hrs by the church in the heart of the so-called red light district; so far, so good. Usually, our days in this beautiful city consisted only of 'window shopping'; it was fascinating to walk the red light district – eye-opening, in fact!

At 1300hrs, I arrived at our pre-determined rendezvous (after a morning's walk around the sights), but there was no sign of Tul. I returned to our hotel but was told he'd left a few hours ago, so I set off on an afternoon-long search for my elusive friend. At about 2230hrs, I decided to return to the digs. As I negotiated the throngs of people on my way back, I heard the undisputed, though obviously pissed, Northern Irish tones of Ian George Tully: 'Hey Scriv, over here! I'm here, you silly twat, where y' been?'

He was fucking stoned, having obviously taken the opportunity to sample more than a couple of 'brownies'. Back in our room, he decided to light a joint we'd purchased a day or two earlier. After a couple of drags, he started doing the fucking sack race around the room, using his pillowcase. That didn't go down too well with the management!

Once, during a trip to Cyprus, we were out dining one evening. I made the mistake of telling Tul that not only did I fancy one of the waitresses, but I was going to 'pull' her. I was, back in the day, very confident of my ability to 'score'. Tul – the twat – thought otherwise!

The waitress strode to our table and asked what drinks we wanted. I ordered a beer... and Tul, in a very camp voice, asked for a cocktail. She returned with my beer and his ridiculous-looking, literally flaming, cocktail. 'Have a lovely evening, boys, and a great night together,' she whispered with a wink at Mr Tully! She never gave me a second look. Cheers, Tul. He was pissing himself as we made an early exit!

Whilst on the beach one day, I buried my trainers for safe keeping whilst we were in the sea. Trying to find them afterwards, however, proved too difficult a task. Whatever happened to them, I can only hazard an educated guess. And that would be the obvious; they sailed out to sea with the tide!

In Tunisia, we walked into a shop which sold tacky items of every description under the hot sun! The proprietor offered us everything in his little shop if we would give him our Adidas trainers! We politely refused, before doing one!

Tul was fantastic company wherever we went; he made me laugh so much, and it was usually when he was in a mood, like when he wrote an hilarious note in his diary at the depot.

Peter Ralphs, Mick Teece, Tul, Helen Carter and I went to Dublin for just a day. Tul, as usual, sorted the travel arrangements. Arriving in Dublin, however, it was suggested we take a trip south to Avoca, where the television series *Ballykissangel* had been filmed. We got the coastal train to Avoca, then paid a random bloke of mature years to take us, on the back of his flatbed pick-up, to the actual filming location. En-route, he stopped the truck and asked us all to follow him. 'I've something to show you lads,' he said with an excited twinkle in his eye. He walked us to a memorial of sorts and told us very proudly in his wonderful southern accent, that it was in honour of Thomas Moore. Well, without another word from him, I launched into a speech about how Thomas Moore had been a good and trusted friend of King Henry VIII; but a friend who refused to condone the King's proposed divorce from Queen Catherine, his first wife, in order to marry Anne Boleyn. I rambled on, telling them all about the dreadful penalty Thomas Moore paid for his stubbornness. How he was eventually, to the King's regret, charged with Treason, and executed after a show trial in Westminster Hall; even telling my listening audience Thomas's last words: 'I die the King's servant... but God's first.' No-one uttered a word whilst I was talking, but immediately after I stopped, our little Irish 'chauffeur' turned to me and said: 'That was a wonderful story, sir... but this *is not* that Thomas Moore.' Everyone just pissed themselves laughing. Tul sidled up to me and said: 'What a twat you are, Scriv.'

I went on loads of holidays and trips with Tul, and enjoyed every one. Eventually, he decided to return to his home city. The peace treaty had been agreed and signed, so now Belfast was a safe place to live again. He got himself a flat, and a position with Ulsterbus, and he was very happy. He invited me over for a few days, and during my stay he took me on lots of drives to show me the sights of 'the Troubles'. It all fascinated me. Seeing it for real was a whole lot different to television footage. But for me, and I'll always be grateful for this, the best part of the whole holiday was Tul taking me to the house that my football idol, the late George Best had grown up in. He also took me on the very route of the football legend's funeral procession to Stormont, where the service had taken place. We even walked up the steps and peered inside. And to cap the day, Tul took me to George's resting place in Roslyn Cemetery. I purchased flowers on the way, which I left on the grave. Fittingly, it seemed, as I had flown in to George Best Airport at the start of a few days with my mate in Belfast, and that was fascinating, too.

Our recently-created office positions involved a spell of driving as and when required. On one of these days, Tul was operating a 42 service between Wellington and the Woodside estate (via Telford bus station). I was working in Bob's former office, which Tul and I had made our own (our desks butted up so we were facing one another, me looking out towards the traffic office), when Peter walked in. He said I needed to go with him to the bus station information office as there was a gentleman in there complaining about a driver, and he was becoming aggressive and irate! The people who worked in the information office should have been able to deal with the complaint; nevertheless, Peter and I drove to Telford. Upon our arrival at the Traveline office, we found all the staff on their own side of the counter, and a very distressed young man pacing up and down on the customer side. After a quick chat with the staff, it became apparent that Ian Tully was the driver whom the gentleman was complaining about. He was driving one of the 'Noddy' buses on service 42.

This is how the conversation between Peter (initially) and the upset young man went:

'Good morning, sir, I am the manager; could you explain to me what your complaint is please; would you like a glass of water?'

'No.'

He was kind of sobbing, I suppose, making odd-sounding noises which continued as he tried to tell us what had so upset him. By this time, I had walked into the area where the public had access to the counter. You will have to use your imagination here; try to picture the scene: here is a young man walking around sobbing and sucking in air as he explained that as the bus pulled up, the driver (Tul) opened the door. The intending passenger had a pushchair (complete with baby) and was in the process of putting it on the bus, when apparently the driver closed the door, causing damage to the pushchair, which rendered it useless. The complainant, however, put it another way, between his sobs:

'I tried to put the pushchair on the bus, but the driver shut the doors on it... and now it's fucked!'

'Sir,' said Peter, a little shocked, 'do try to tell us without using foul and abusive language. I completely understand you are upset, but nevertheless...'

I was just beginning to see the funny side (rightly or wrongly) when the lad's response to Peter's attempt to cool the situation brought the following (in between sobs and sharp intakes of breath), which caused me and a few others to burst our sides in uncontrollable laughter:

'The door opened, and I tried to put the babby on the bus, and the driver shut the door on the pushchair and the babby. And now it's F-U-C-K-E-DEED!' He spelt it out because Peter told him not to swear. An absolute classic! Then to cap it all, he added: 'And Stubley's is shut on a Wednesday.'

Well, this comment completely brought the house down. Stubley's, back in the 1990s, was a junk shop of sorts in Wellington, near the depot, where you could buy almost anything on the cheap. It was very different, however, on the last occasion that I was in there; it now sells high-quality items of furniture and the like.

The matter was eventually resolved when Peter agreed to compensate the lad for the damage to the 'babby's' pushchair. And Ian Tully escaped with just a berating from the boss, as I remember.

Tul made me laugh many times without even trying; I loved working with him, and our occasional holidays or outings. We went to Prague for a few days with one of Tul's mates, and a fellow busman, John Percy Hughes. And being in this crazy industry, we decided to sample all the various forms of public transport on offer in the beautiful city. We bought our tickets not realising that we had to 'validate' them on each ride we took. One morning, towards the end of our stay, we boarded the train into the centre as per usual. As we alighted onto the platform, we were individually 'rushed' by a group of armed police or soldiers, who pushed us up against a wall, put a gun in our faces, and demanded to see our tickets. When we produced them, we were told in extremely vicious fashion that we hadn't validated them. We were forced to pay a hefty fine or go to prison for seven days! Prague is the cleanest city I have ever visited... but I would never go back there again, simply for the way we were treated at the train station.

Just after arriving at our digs in Prague, we all met up in the garden (of sorts), after freshening up. Actually, it was quite a large area of tables and chairs which stood under rattan canopies. After ordering drinks, we decided to have something to eat. Unfortunately, the menu was written in Czech, but it was fun to watch Tul and John trying to decide what to order. They had a difference of opinion as to what one dish on the menu actually was! Tul insisted it was the same dish (not intending to order; they were just trying some 'one-upmanship') that was being devoured by about eight people at a nearby table. In order to settle the argument, Tul called over the waitress and pointed to the menu, and then to the nearby table, which had what looked like a piglet on it, which the people were carving from. The waitress simply smiled, nodded, and (as far as we were concerned) went on with her duties. Tul puffed his chest out to John, who readily accepted defeat. Presently, the waitress appeared again, carrying a cooked animal of some kind, and proceeded to put it in front of Tul, along with a knife and fork! It was absolutely hilarious; the waitress obviously thought that Tul was ordering the same as what the eight or so people on the nearby table were eating... between them! 'You two will have to help me out here,' said Tul, instead of returning it to the kitchen as a mistaken order. We left him to it as we had each ordered a sandwich!

One morning, after Tul had again fallen victim to Peter's wrath, I reminded him that it was the anniversary of his joining the company. He wasn't in the best of moods, understandably. And as I was talking to him (across our desks), he looked at me, then grabbed his large A4 diary and began scribbling – in large capitals – on the page 'EIGHT YEARS AT THIS POXY SHITHOLE', or words to that effect. I was pissing myself again! A little while later, Peter came in and asked Tul to go to Morrison's for the bacon baps, which we had on most mornings if we didn't go to the Little Chef. We took it in turn to pay. And whilst he was out, Peter noticed Tul's diary open on his desk (no, I did not point it out to him)... fortunately, the boss saw the funny side as well.

Tul and I were both free in our personal lives to do as we pleased; no commitments to a marriage for either of us, so we decided to enjoy life as and when the opportunities came along. I can't now remember the timeline of our adventures, but they were regular, and meticulously planned by my great friend.

He joined the industry, after following his dad Billy into it (as my youngest son Tom followed me, spending ten years of his working life at National Express), and after all these years, I can say with certainty, you will not meet anyone who has a bad word to say about Ian Tully. And his knowledge of the industry is up there with the best! These days, Tul is coach driving again, as he was before the Covid-19 pandemic struck.

We had planned to walk the Hadrian's Wall path in 2021, and had got into a brilliant routine of meeting up in Shifnal every Sunday morning to walk for at least three hours as part of our training. Tul said he would organise our agenda, and I promised to meet the majority of the cost. I was so looking forward to it. I had it in mind to get as much sponsorship as I could because I am part of a group called Minton Memories which, as I write, is committed to raising sufficient funds to place a bust of the person (my late great friend and mentor, Mr Bill Williams BEM, mentioned earlier) as a lasting memorial in respect and admiration of a lifetime of tireless voluntary work for (amongst other worthy causes) socially deprived children.

Unfortunately, however, Tul and I had a bit of a fall-out, which scuppered our intended walk in the north of England. In an effort to make contact again, I wrote to Tul at Shrewsbury, his then depot base. He did eventually reply by email, outlining how hurt he was about my Facebook posts regarding our fall-out. I emailed back explaining that because he had chosen to prevent me from contacting him via the usual methods, I had to do something to get his attention. I received one (seemingly) final message from him, which omitted to say whether or not he still regarded us as friends.

I'm very happy to say now, however, that after bumping into each other in Llandudno in May 2022, we resolved our differences, and we are now good friends again... if we ever were not!

In March 1998, Peter Ralphs was still Garage Manager when, as one of his two duty managers, I took a call from a man with a definite Aussie accent. He introduced himself as a member of the production team of the Australian 'soap' *Home and Away*. Of course, I immediately began to listen with mounting interest, in an effort to identify the prankster; but it was no prank! The gentleman on the other end of the line explained that the programme was coming to Ironbridge near Madeley 'in your beautiful neck of the woods' to film an episode. As the conversation progressed, it transpired that he wanted to film a scene involving the character 'Selina', and one of our buses! I asked him to hold the line whilst I spoke to the depot manager. When I popped into Pete's office and told him about the call I was on, he rolled back in his very comfortable chair... and pissed himself laughing. I eventually convinced him that the caller was genuine, and he gave me permission to continue. As I was going through the door, Peter said (in his very posh accent), 'Why don't you ask if you can be in the scene? After all, it's our bus they want in it.'

The telephone chat ended with the caller thanking me for our positive response and he said we would all (Peter, Tul and me) be invited to breakfast with the cast at Sutton Maddock very soon. When I related all the details to Tul, he said, 'I'll drive the bus, Scriv.' I agreed; then at the first opportunity, I asked one of the H&A team if I could be in the scene. He kindly replied in the affirmative, much to my astonishment!

On the day the episode was filmed, with Tul driving into Ironbridge from Madeley Bank, I was standing at the bus stop with a couple of the cast. Other members alighted, and then we boarded, and Tul did the business as the scene played out; driving out of shot and down to the car park. Job done: all happy, and Tul and I ever qualified to say that we were in an episode of *Home and Away*.

Thank you for your friendship, Tul, mate.

Chapter Six

Final Years at
Wonderful Wellington

In the late 1990s, Tul went to work at Shrewsbury Depot. I missed him on a daily basis, but got stuck into my management duties. By this time, Nick Newcombe had arrived at the depot, under the title of General Manager. One of his first actions was to promote me to the position of Traffic Manager in April 1999, giving me full authority to deal with the drivers, and the running of the depot on a day-to-day basis.

In October 1998, I had attended my second course; an 'Interviewing Skills' forum, for which I was presented with another certificate, this time by Anica Goodwin (Personnel Skills Manager, so the certificate said; she was the HRM, actually). Much was being made about courses and accumulating certificates at that time, so the more the merrier, I suppose. And it proved its worth on numerous occasions, as my career rolled on.

The following year (in August), I made a decision at a driver's Formal Conduct Hearing, which brought about my second appearance (on behalf of the company) at an Industrial Tribunal Hearing, held in Shrewsbury. I was attending (as I had in the first instance) as the 'dismissing officer'. The hearing revolved around the driver's complaint that I had treated him more severely than another driver for a similar offence; the offence being a constant failure to adhere to the company's policy regarding the paying in of daily fare-takings. The driver had been treated fairly, as his conduct record proved.

The tribunal found in the company's favour, therefore justifying my decision to dismiss (as in the previous case).

I don't wish to sound harsh, or cocky, but I had no problem dismissing drivers for offences which warranted the severest 'award'. And looking back on all of those decisions, I would do the same again.

During Nick Newcombe's time as General Manager, and after he had concluded a Conduct Hearing brought about by my investigation as Traffic Manager into a ticketing offence, he came into my office and said sarcastically (because he hadn't wanted to make the decision, he actually had no option but to do otherwise), 'When they write the history of this company, your name will be up there in neon lights.' I replied, 'Yes, and for the right reasons, Nick.'

We had a small outstation at Bridgnorth, and one day one of the drivers informed me that a colleague was apparently stealing diesel fuel from the depot. I've never been one to listen to 'tittle tattle', but said I would put a notice in the depot.

The notice, according to the same informant, hadn't made a scrap of difference, so this time he gave me a name. I asked him if his information was certain, and he told me it was. I decided to visit the depot at the end of the driver's shift, to see for myself whether there was a case of stealing happening at Bridgnorth.

I then went to see Nick Newcombe, to advise him of what the informant had told me, and of my intended plan to deal with it. He agreed, after I reminded him that a notice warning that possible disciplinary action would be taken if the practice did not cease. 'Okay, go ahead,' was his response.

I checked the Bridgnorth rota in order to set a date for my surprise visit, and on the appointed evening I drove to Bridgnorth and parked my car a little way from the outstation. On entering the depot, I found myself a position where I could observe the fuel pump without being seen myself. The driver duly arrived and drove onto the pump. He then proceeded to fuel his bus; all well and good so far. But then, having filled the bus, he drove it off the pump (leaving the nozzle dangling), and brought his car to the pump, where he inserted the nozzle and began fuelling his car! I made my way to him as he was filling in the fuel sheet. His face was a picture. He tried to say that he only took enough fuel to get him home, as his car was empty. I asked him to switch the ignition on. He did so, and it registered a full tank! As he had recorded all the fuel for the bus, on the fuel sheet, it didn't take a member of Mensa to realise what was going on. I told him what a bloody idiot I thought he was, and he sheepishly agreed. I then took note of the fuel pump total, and the fuel sheet total (which should normally record a similar amount to the previous day's use, as the bus had operated on the same duty), before asking him to present himself at Wellington depot at 1000hrs the following morning. I advised him that it would be in his interests to attend so that he might explain his actions; the result of which may lead to a formal disciplinary hearing, conducted by the general manager. We never saw that driver again, which was a shame to be honest because aside from that (or those) transgressions, he had been a model employee. Some might see my actions as 'entrapment', but one has to realise that outstation drivers were trusted to safeguard the company's property at all times; as was everyone else, of course.

We had a policy which allowed drivers to wear shorts; proper 'trouser' type shorts, during the summer months. After a while, however, a small number of drivers decided to take the piss by arriving for work in colourful Bermuda shorts (one in particular came in swimming shorts, with sandals or slip-on type beach footwear). I posted a notice reminding drivers of the agreement and their responsibility to adhere to it. I added that the concession would be 'reviewed' if this practice continued. It did continue, so I banned the wearing of shorts and unsuitable footwear. I rang John Morrow and told him of my decision, and the reason. 'Well done,' he said, 'we'll make it policy.' This decision was to come back and bite me further along the line of my career in this crazy industry!

The end of the year was also the end of the decade, the century, and indeed the millennium. What a great time to be a member of the world's population. I was forty-six years old and in the prime of life. I had two great sons, and an ex-wife who was and has remained one of my best friends. I was enjoying my job, and although my time with the Longmynd Adventure Camp was now over, John Preece (an almost life-long friend; Kenny Turner holds that title) and I had permission to continue camping on a part of the land which the LAC (in its early years as the WVS Boys Camp) had been allowed to use, in Minton, Shropshire.

Towards the end of 1999, I received a phone call from John Morrow. He said that the company was worried about possible computer glitches occurring on 'Millennium Night', as he so charmingly put it. He went on to say that someone (perhaps a driver) 'might be willing to forego the celebrations to stay on the end of the phone should anything odd happen to the computers etc, at the turn of the most important hour of all our lives'. How delightfully dramatic! What, I wondered, could the volunteer do in the unlikely event of Morrow's fears being realised? He asked me to post a notice in the drivers' room, asking for a volunteer. I was quite prepared to do this until he added that the volunteer would receive four hundred pounds tax-free for giving up his/her celebration plans. I agreed to write the notice, and the call ended with John saying he would be in touch in a couple of days.

There was no way a notice was going to be posted! The new millennium celebrations meant little or nothing to me: I certainly wasn't going out on the piss. Plus, Tul's and my plans to spend 'Millennium Night' at Sydney Harbour had well and truly been sunk!

Morrow rang me again as promised, eagerly awaiting a positive response from me. I told him with heavy heart (yeah, right) that I hadn't managed to persuade anyone to do the deed. Before he could comment, I said, 'John, I'll do it for you, mate. I was going out but it's okay, I'll cancel and do the night watchman task.' 'You sure, Scriv; you don't mind, really?' 'No John, don't worry, I'll do it.'

He was like a dog with two... bones. 'Thank you very much, Scriv, that's a weight off my mind... and I'll sanction the four hundred quid the second this conversation is over; thanks again, mate, you're a diamond.'

It was the softest, easiest money I have ever 'earned' during all my working years... so far!

I apologise now to everyone who was at Wellington Depot at the time for not giving them the opportunity... but in a similar scenario, would they have acted in the same fashion? I think they might have.

'Millennium Night' came and went, with no hint of a problem with anything; certainly not with the beers I was necking at home. Cheers, Mr Morrow.

I had no idea at this point that my thirteen-year stay at wonderful Wellington was coming to an end. I loved the depot, the town – everything – even the walks to and from Dawley. I had a lovely two-bed ground-floor flat with a front and rear garden, and my own garage. Plus, I had plenty of female company. What could possibly be better than that set of life's gifts? Nothing, as it turned out!

Even as a manager, I think I retained the friendship, if not the respect (or should that be the other way round?), of most of my colleagues. People like Dave Richards and his son Dale (whom I was destined to work with again at Shrewsbury), Colin Turner, his brother John, Bill Parton, Andy Winton, Steve

Paskin, Nick McDowell, Mark Frost, Mick 'Buster' Edwards, Pete Small, Wilbur Bruck, and his brother George (what characters they were); Dave and Mick Thomas, John Hodges, Kenny Rogers, John Edge, Sean Owen and his wife Christine. Her father Dai Williams, John Holmes, Doug Pomeroy, Billy Tully, Ray Slyde, C.A. Davies and his brother Ken. Stuart Peters, Steve Paskin, Kevin Bradburn, Gurwinder Jandhu, Terry Vickery, Jeremy Kenny, Steve Hall, Bob Richardson, Derek Worrall, Lee Reynolds, Mel Gough, Dave and Hazel Skitt, Derek Summers, Winston Law, and his son David. Also at the depot during my time were Eddie Tompson, Sandra Price, Colin and Jenny Davies, Edwin Managh, Charlie Davis, Charlie Bailey, Maureen Wishart, her sister, Sandra Price, Michelle Hall, Tim Brittain, Don and Sam Bates, Harry Singh, Dennis, Charlie and Mick McLafferty, Jim Churm, Terry Hassall, Steve Ellis and his (then) wife Teresa (now Budgen), Steve Partington, John Morgan, Reece Hunt, Stan Robinson, Sonia Macken, Martin Jay, John Salter, Tim Hull, Tim Clay, Jim Edmunds, Chris Probert, Neil Davies and his best buddy Derek Briarwood. It was a big depot with a large fleet, which required a full company of drivers, engineers, office and cleaning staff, such as Alan Edwards, his mother Gill, and Kathy Smith. On the drivers list we can also add Richard Bradshaw, Rupert Collier, Frank Sobczuk, Tommy Riggs, Keith Danks, Keith Cotterill, Steve Griffiths, Don and Rob Housden, Chris Jones, Paul Giles, Geoff Peate, Dave Porter, Pete and Debbie Ashford, and Neil Law. Some former colleagues declined my invitation of a mention, but sincere apologies to anyone I've unwittingly forgotten to include.

John Davies (he called everyone 'friend') was the very capable Engineering Manager, aided and abetted by Arthur Pemberton, John Peters, Brian Jones, John Trubshaw, Roy Turner and Roger Vaughan amongst others, i.e. Cyril the bodyman, Dave Hipkiss, James Turner, and John Marston. Roger Vaughan was a straight-talking guy whom you either loved or didn't. I loved.

A welcome feature of Midland Red North, certainly during the middle to late 1990s was the periodical staff magazine (as mentioned previously). It included reports from our sister depots; the odd funny story... and a message from the MD, Trevor Petty. In the 1996 Christmas edition, he writes about the company improving the quality of the network, and how 'pleasant and welcoming drivers; and clean punctual buses will be our main weapon, in ensuring a competitor does not succeed'. The Wacky Races spring to mind!

Page five was devoted to 'Changing Times at Telford'. Monday 4th November saw the biggest reorganisation of the town's services 'for many years'. The new town was made up from a number of smaller towns and villages, including Dawley, Wellington, Oakengates, Madeley, Trench, Hadley and Donnington; all of which were busy old communities now coming under the wing of Telford Development Corporation. New residential areas were built, i.e. Woodside, Brookside, Hollinswood, Stirchley, Randlay, Leegomery and Sutton Hill; and also business areas to offer employment, such as Stafford Park, Horton Wood, and Halesfield. All of these places already had a bus service, but an overhaul was thought necessary by 'the suits'.

One of the biggest drawbacks to this was the free car parks in and around the town centre; so I suppose it was a case of 'Hobson's choice', really: MRN had to make the services more appealing to the majority...car drivers! And by and large, it has to be said, I suppose, that the company succeeded.

'Charlie', the 1920s replica Charabanc which resided at Wellington Depot, was very busy at the time of the service changes; moving around all the areas MRN served, with staff handing out leaflets, and general information regarding the changes.

On another theme, John Trubshaw wrote on Page seven: 'Places have been secured on a course considered appropriate to enable engineering staff to maintain more vehicles at less cost on a shorter timescale. These courses will be held at the headquarters of the Magic Circle, under the instruction of the late Tommy Cooper'. What was the message here, you may well ask!

It was around this time that Colin Turner, Dennis McLafferty and I, amongst others, organised the sponsored bus pull (around the 2/12 'Wacky' route) in aid of the Marelle Rowland Appeal (to raise funds to send a blind Telford baby to America for a sight-saving operation), as mentioned earlier.

Of course, our bus took a very long time to complete its fifteen-mile (approx.) journey. But on a serious note, bus drivers do their very best to keep to their appointed time schedules. Pulling out of bus stops, however, can sometimes take an age, adding precious minutes to the journey, and this problem was brought to light in a poem on page eight of the June 1997 *BUSiness* magazine:

Spare a thought for the Bus Driver
You see me as you drive to work, on much congested road,
I'd done three hours then you know, with ever-growing load.
And though you curse my size and space, I've still got a role to fill:
If all my passengers drove cars - a bigger problem still!
There was a time - you may recall, when we outnumbered you, and cars were mostly owned by those we called "well to do".
The buses and the tramcars too, were filled throughout the day
And you could travel anywhere, without too much to pay.
Well now those days have gone my friend, and most buy cars instead,
And through my windscreen I survey a sea of cars ahead.
And yet my schedules still remain; my watch, a constant foe,
My passengers may miss their train, because the bus was too slow!

So if you see me at a 'stop'; flashing to pull out,
I need to go most urgently, of this there is no doubt!
So please slow down and let me go; your good deed for the day,
It really helps, enormously... to send me on my way.

Those wise words were attributed to Mr David Lloyd. Well done, mate; and very apt!

In the same edition, an amusing article written by yours truly made page seven. Here is the gist of it:

STOWAWAY
A Report of Fare Evasion From Alan Scriven

Hazel Mors was operating the 15:50 hrs 892 service from Wellington to Shifnal, having just terminated as an 892 from Wolverhampton. A lady passenger whispered into Hazel's ear "there's a mouse running about on your bus."

Hazel burst out laughing. "I'm not joking" said the lady, "its grey with sticky up ears."

The lady alighted at Leegomery and Hazel continued on her journey. A little while later the bus was in 'uproar' as everyone was shouting "mouse", and jumping up on the seats!

Upon arrival at the town centre bus station, Dave Richards boarded. Asking everyone to alight, he searched the saloon to no avail. "You'd better report it to the depot" he advised Hazel.

I answered the call and laughed uncontrollably as she told the 'tail'. Dave came on the line saying that fifteen drivers had lost mileage trying to find "this damn mouse".

An emergency request for cheese was put out.................

The incident was eventually resolved when it was considered by all that the tiny freeloader had jumped off, deciding to continue his journey on paw! Hazel set off again.

Interestingly, Phil Evans, who worked in the information office told Dave that a young man had been in a while earlier, *asking how he could get to Shrewsbury, as he needed to take his box full of mice, to sell at a pet shop in the county town. And this was, he said, about the time Hazel departed the bus station. At that time, anyone wishing to travel to Shrewsbury from Telford would have had to change at Wellington! Problem solved.........*

Well apparently not; the following day passengers on the exact same bus were 'up in arms' over a mouse scurrying about..................obviously trying to get the best out of his 'Explorer Ticket'.

Great stories like this were the source of much banter in bus drivers' canteens... including the so called 'Death Cell', as our restroom in Telford Bus Station was referred to by Kenny Parker. Well, it was a very small room with no windows!

The man who chose the title 'the *BUSiness*' for our magazine, Keith Cowey, sadly lost his fight against lung cancer on 30th March 1997. Messages of sympathy went out to his wife Lorraine, and the family. God bless you, Keith.

If memory serves, it was in August 1999 that Arriva, amongst other companies, began working on the Virgin music festivals on the Earl of Bradford's Estate, Weston Park, at Weston-under-Lizard, on the A5 near the A41 junction.

To be fair, it was great fun taking part in ferrying the festival-goers from Wolverhampton and Stafford train stations to Weston Park, a little west of Ivetsey Bank.

John Morrow organised us, inasmuch as deciding who was working from where. I was Traffic Manager at Wellington, and my bus was a Leyland 'Dominant' or 'Tiger' (ugh) from that depot, but people were drafted in from all over the network, as were the buses. One would therefore get the chance to meet up with friends from elsewhere on the patch; great fun for the whole of the weekend, and we were handsomely paid for the privilege!

The task, for most of us, began in earnest on the Saturday morning when the 'outside drivers' were instructed as to which route to operate on, although having said that, it was quite obvious that Stafford drivers would operate the Stafford run, and Cannock would cover Wolverhampton. I worked between Wolverhampton and Weston Park in 1999. So off to the train station, where you would join the queue of buses waiting to load up with (mainly) young, free and single people, all of one mind: to have a fantastic weekend of great music, drinking, dancing, and whatever else they got up to! A few buses were put to work on the Friday to take the 'early birds' to the show.

At about 1600 hrs on the Saturday afternoon, we, or most of us, would be 'stood down', having ferried all the travelling folk from and to the venue. I drove my bus home (with John's permission) and left it near to my flat in Chiltern Gardens. Then following a well-earned break, we would drive to Weston Park to begin taking the 'one-day' revellers back to the train station. Some would be at the concert for the whole duration; walking off the accommodation fields on Monday morning in various states of consciousness, and dress, as they struggled to hold on to whatever possessions they could manage to carry; never the small tents they brought with them, however, or the empty beer bottles and cans, etc; they would be left to an army of volunteers drafted in on the Monday afternoon to clear up the considerable amount of litter caused by a three-day event.

On Sunday morning, it would be a case of 'ferrying' passengers to and from the venue on a continuous roll; brilliant fun, which all of us enjoyed. I learned a couple of days ago from Colin Turner that apparently Morrow would open up the boot of his company car at various stages throughout the day, and drivers would help themselves to the ample amounts of food stored in it. He never once, however, invited me to indulge!

They were long days, but brilliant. On Monday morning, we would be required only to return the (mainly) youngsters back to their respective railway stations. This would begin very early in the morning, and go on until late afternoon. Drivers would be asked to keep returning to Weston Park until everyone had departed the fields.

For V99, John Morrow gave us all strict instructions on how to operate the one-way system he had 'designed' for arriving at, and leaving, the drop-off point.

Better organisation prevailed the following year, regarding the pick-up and drop-off points, because we had use of a piece of land big enough to set down and board our passengers.

V99 was succeeded by the so called 'V00 Do' year... V2000. This was my final year of working on the festival runs, sadly.

Chapter Seven

Returning to Cannock

The new millennium began without any fuss. Predicted problems with the computers, etc., never materialised, and business went on as per usual. I had struck up a good working relationship with Nick Newcombe, who by and large left the day-to-day running of the depot to me, with regard to the drivers. Nick was a jovial guy, who betrayed the reputation that preceded him. Some thought he had – up to joining us – been a strict boss who stood for nothing. He was quite the opposite, actually. If anything was kicking off anywhere, he would ask me either to accompany him to wherever the scene was being played out, or just send me to deal with it. I was fine with that. Another person whom I had a deep respect for was Hazel Skitt. She held the position of Union Liaison Officer at one point (after Richie Benting left the company) during our time at that great depot, so we saw plenty of each other, owing to our respective positions. Hazel was good at her job, and very fair. She would fight tooth and nail for whoever she was defending at a formal disciplinary hearing, if she considered the driver was innocent. On the other hand, if evidence showed the 'defendant' to be guilty, she would advise him/her to accept the 'award' handed out by management.

We even went on holiday together. Hazel, her husband Dave and two of their children were invited, along with Tina and me, our son Tom, and his then girlfriend Lisa, to spend some time in Crete, organised by (the now late) driver Bob Jones and his lovely wife. For some reason, Bob had apparently previously informed our hosts in Crete that his first name was actually

Merlin. Whether it was or not, I can't say, but it was comical to see his lady wife walking up and down the little bus which carried us from the airport to our digs, asking everyone to refer to and call Bob 'Merlin' as soon as we arrived. To his credit, Dave Skitt never faltered, but I and others called Bob by his known name on almost every occasion. My son Tom, always one for extracting the urine and looking for a laugh (wonder where he gets these qualities from), mischievously called him 'Bob' whenever our hosts were in earshot! And if 'Merlin' purposely ignored him, hoping Tom would get the 'message', he was proved wrong every time; Tom would simply say it louder. Great fun, especially as Bob's wife would throw looks to kill in Tom's direction.

I took my ex-wife Tina as a thank you for all the times she was happy for me to go to Camp whilst we were married. It was her first time abroad, and she, along with all of us, thoroughly enjoyed it. My thanks to Mr and Mrs Jones for their kind invitation to join in such a wonderful experience – if you discount the occasion of Tina and Lisa being groped by a couple of youths, as they rode past on motorcycles near our digs on the beach!

On 2nd April, I was presented with yet another certificate, this one for 'Completing Awareness Training in the Conduct Procedure'. It would come in very useful, as things turned out! But before that there was the small business of my attendance at a meeting called by Wrockwardine Wood and Trench Parish Council. Members of the public had apparently asked for the meeting with the councillors and a representative from Arriva, after service changes were introduced on 14th February 2000.

The *Shropshire Star*, on Wednesday 15th March, quoted me as saying the following:

"We are a company and cannot operate without profit. We were losing three per cent of our passengers annually and so were forced to make these changes to avoid going out of

business. Telford was built for the motor car, and there are simply not enough people using certain bus routes for them to remain viable."

Vice-Chair Councillor Charles Smith said: "some residents were being made prisoners by the changes, especially pensioners."

The report closed with: *Mr Scriven agreed that the changes did not suit everyone, and said he would take the comments back to Arriva.*

But at the same time, I knew full well that it wouldn't make a scrap of difference!

The early part of the New Year brought about a massive change in my career, and that of others. I never saw it coming, but I was about to end my days at wonderful Wellington; retracing my steps back to Cannock after thirteen or so glorious years, when I had left to start what I (and everyone else who joined me) thought would be a career at our new Walsall depot... lol.

John Morrow arrived at Wellington and told Nick and me that a 'management restructure' was to take place. All of us in management positions throughout the network would be invited to apply for the up-and-coming new positions. The existing Garage Manager and Traffic Manager positions were to be got rid of in favour of a 'new-look team', which would set each depot up as follows:

1) Passenger Service Manager to replace Garage Manager.
2) Staff Manager to replace Traffic Manager.

Added to this would be the position of Staff Supervisor, and a number of driver-clerks (depending on the size of the depot).

As well as this, there would be 'further opportunities to progress with the company', which John told us would be in the form of senior positions such as Operations Manager, based at Head Office (Cannock) and taking control of an 'area'.

To cut a long story short, I was informed by JM after the

relevant interviews that I had been successful, and would take over Cannock Depot (the poisoned chalice) as PSM, and Nick Newcombe would become Operations Manager. This promotion most definitely put Kevin Walker's nose out of joint! He was sure he was going to get the job; not because he was one of Morrow's best friends, and a fellow Birmingham City Football Club supporter – no, he was very good at his job, was Kevin, or so I was told... and a nice bloke to boot!

Actually, and in hindsight (which we've all got degrees in), I should have stayed at Wellington. The problem with that, though, was that anyone who was a part of the management sector was expected to apply for more senior vacancies; if you didn't, in the eyes of the 'powers that be', it was a message that you didn't wish to progress with your career! I only wish that my promotion to PSM could have been at Wellington, because I feel certain that if that had been the case, I would still be at the depot today, albeit the new one on Stafford Park, Telford, which replaced the old place we all loved!

I said my sad goodbyes (to anyone that seemed sad to see me leave), and cleared my desk. The next phase of my working life would soon be underway.

Upon arrival at my new depot in early May 2000, I discovered that my staff had already been selected. This was contrary to what I had understood from John Morrow. He assured me at the interview that (if I was successful) I would have a say in who was appointed to what position. As it turned out, Brian Campbell was to be my Staff Manager, and Melvyn Westwood was in as Staff Supervisor, with (the now late) Clive Bevington; Derek Franks and Craig Woods being my duty clerks. A lovely lady called Carol Wallwork, who was already working in the traffic office, completed our team. Carol was extremely good at what she did, and a pleasure to work with.

I knew Brian quite well, and I had worked with his wife Jayne at Wellington; he is a great bloke, and I like him a lot. We worked well together. Brian was also the management shop steward. A funny story involving Brian was the time when we took Ken Gough, a retiring driver, out to lunch (normal procedure), with the union chief Norman Ashmore. Norman was a nice, even-tempered and reasonable chap; we never had a cross word... even at the wage negotiation meetings in my office. At these meetings (as with Wellington whenever I was asked to manage, or take part in them), I would always ensure that light refreshments were provided. When the Garage Union Committee entered my office, the Liaison Officer would pass me a piece of paper with their 'ideals' written on it. Invariably, I would take one look at it then stand up, walk round to the refreshment table, and cover the food with tea-towels before opening my office door and saying: 'Good day, folks, come back when you have more realistic suggestions.' A deal would always be thrashed out eventually and they always appreciated the 'ice-breaking' intention on my part.

On the day that we took Ken out for lunch, after the traditional 'bus pull'[4], I sat in the passenger seat and Brian drove the car, with Norman and Ken occupying the rear seats. After a very nice couple of hours at the Tumbledown pub (if memory serves), I decided to travel back in the nearside rear seat, with our retiring colleague beside me. We arrived back at Cannock Depot, and Norman brought the car to a halt outside the Traffic office. About six drivers were milling about as Brian got out, leaving me to slide the front seat forward in order to get myself out. Unfortunately, the seat refused to slide forward more than a few inches, so I had to try and get my body through the smallest gap one could imagine. Ultimately, I found myself wedged half inside and half

---

[4]Whenever a driver retired, it was the custom to attach a rope on the front of the bus and then the managers and union reps, and maybe one or two drivers, would pull the bus towards the gates: great fun. Ken Gough's retirement, however, was the only one I was ever involved with. Maybe they'll do it for me at Select when I retire?

outside of the car… with my staff manager Norman, Ken, and all the bystanders pissing themselves laughing! Even I saw the funny side of it… eventually!

Brian Campbell had told me that I was coming to the depot with 'a bit of a reputation'. 'Regarding what?' I enquired. He said that my apparent reputation for being strict had all but set everyone against me, even before I took my jacket off on my first day. I responded to this by saying that as long as my office team understood that they mustn't keep anything from me regarding the depot's day-to-day operations, we would get along fine. As for the driving staff, I said that they could judge me as we went along. And judge me they did! Colin Mathews (who sadly passed away in October 2022), one of the long-serving drivers, absolutely refused to speak to me. In fact, the man never spoke a single word to me during my time at the depot. Years after I had moved on, however – or to put it as it actually was, had been moved on – if I saw him on the road, he would always acknowledge me; even have a conversation with me if our paths crossed in Cannock Bus Station, or the shopping centre. Very strange! To his credit, whilst we were both at Cannock, he had the gall, or the brass neck, or the bollocks, to ignore me to my face after I had said good morning to him once… I only ever said it once. God bless you, Colin; rest in peace. Colin was well known for dressing up as Santa during the festive season. In point of fact, quite a few drivers did that; Ade Duvall (ex-Cannock, now employed at Select) and Mick Teece from wonderful Wellington, for instance.

Neil Barker was the young MD at this point, and he had the final say, I suppose, on who went where, if anywhere, as a result of the reorganisation I mentioned earlier. I found Neil to be difficult (at least some of the time) if I'm honest. I managed to get myself firmly into his bad books whilst I was still at Wellington.

Kevin Bellfield (Commercial Director) rang me one Monday morning. He told me that a complaint had been lodged against one of our drivers (the now late Gareth Williams). The complainant alleged that Gareth had 'left him standing' by operating the service early on the previous Sunday afternoon, in Ironbridge, Telford. I promised to investigate. And following a full investigation, which included twice interviewing Gareth, and intensely studying all the relevant data from his day's work, I found absolutely nothing to suggest that Gareth had done anything other than exactly what the running board for that particular duty had directed him to do.

I rang Kevin back and informed him of the results of my investigation. He seemed to accept what I told him... but within the hour, I received a call from Neil Barker. He was not pleased; he said the complainant was going to inform the Ombudsman, and this meant 'big trouble' for the company. He told me, in no uncertain words, to review everything, and get back to him. My reply to this demand from Neil went so much against the grain that the MD hardly ever spoke to me again! I said: 'With respect, Neil [first mistake], the complainant informing the Ombudsman would only mean big trouble if our driver had not done his job properly. Furthermore, I have thoroughly investigated every aspect of this person's complaint, and there is not one scrap of evidence to even suggest that our driver ran the service – an irregular Sunday service – early. He did his job and performed his required duties to the letter, and so therefore, I will not be taking this any further... now is there anything else, Mr Barker?' That was my second mistake!

When I say mistake, I simply mean that my answers didn't line up with what he wanted to hear. He put the phone down on me! Next thing, Nick Newcombe and Kevin Bellfield were on my case. I invited them both to check my findings (or lack of) after fully investigating the matter; they did so, and like me, couldn't find anything amiss. End of... Neither I nor the company (as far as I am aware) heard anything more from the complainant, who for my money probably missed the bus through his own stupid fault.

Shortly after the beginning of my relatively short tenure at Cannock Depot, the inter-depot football competition got underway. I had been down to play for Wellington, but because of my new position, I informed the Cannock squad that my loyalty was now to my new depot, and so I would play for them.
'Thanks, but we don't need you, boss; we have a full squad,' I was 'politely' rebuffed! So because I was really looking forward to playing, I rang Mark Frost and said I would play for Wellington, if they still wanted me to. Mark gave me the green light (well, I could play a bit back in the day). It was a five- (or six-) a-side competition and we played against Cannock during the afternoon. They kicked lumps out of me all through the game! We must have done pretty well, however, because I remember lining up with the Wellington lads to be presented with a t-shirt from Neil Barker. As he handed me mine, he said with unmistakeable sarcasm: 'Nothing like a conflict of loyalty, is there?' I ignored him.
Cannock Depot won the competition.
Neil and I are now 'Facebook friends'.

Simon Gray-Davis was hopeful of playing for Cannock, but prior to the competition he had been off work with an arm injury, which was still quite heavily dressed. He came in to see me during the preceding week to say that he was okay to play for Cannock. By this time, I knew I was going to be playing for Wellington... and I also knew how good a player Simon was, both in goal and outfield. He had played in both positions when we – as I mentioned earlier – took on a team from Scotland in the 1990s. There was no way I could allow him to play against my former depot if my current depot didn't want me! I got round it by telling him that he had told me he was unfit for work, and therefore, I explained, he could not unfortunately be considered to take part!

Simon and I have remained friends to this day; in fact, at the time of writing, we are working together again, at Select Bus Services. And as far as I know, he has never held it against me, and that's the mark of a genuine guy, and a true friend, although he reminds me of it at every opportunity! So, very sorry mate, but needs must... To be absolutely honest, though, I don't think I could have allowed him to play, even if we had both been in the same team; not with an injured arm.

I settled into my role as Cannock PSM, and performed my duties as well, and as professionally, as was possible, under the circumstances, which I'll come to a little later.

John Morrow invited me to form a small group of people from around the network, in order to write up the company's new drug and alcohol policy. I felt very honoured, but it was short-lived, as my situation unfolded...

Arriva Head Office shared part of Cannock's depot space in Delta Way, so I felt I was being watched during every minute of the day! I probably wasn't, but on almost every occasion when I was outside, near the Traffic Office I could feel, then see, Head Office staff staring through their upstairs windows... Morrow being one of the most regular.

I remember Nick Newcombe coming to conduct my 'Appraisal Interview' in 2001. At the end of it, he asked me if I had any concerns. I replied with a question: 'About what, Nick?'

'Well, are you happy?'

I probed him with regard to what he meant, exactly, but nothing came out. So I took the bull by the horns, as they say. I told him I wasn't too happy about certain members of Head Office personnel interfering unnecessarily with my depot. Just because HO was situated on Cannock Depot ground didn't mean it was okay or fair for any of them to 'stick their oar in' regularly, in matters concerning the direct operation of the depot. Why would they need or want a depot manager when 'those upstairs' kept interrupting the flow? Well, by this time of course, Newcombe himself was part of that clan, so was probably not best pleased himself to hear that! But he assured me that he 'understood', and even agreed with me.

It wasn't too long, however, after this supposedly confidential chat that I was forced out of Cannock, and packed off to Shrewsbury, then forced out of that depot, too. I'll return to this later.

Shortly after moving to Cannock, I was called up to Head Office by Mike Doyle, the Financial Director. He told me that the (mostly) articulated trucks that parked on my depot yard were subject to a monthly rent, but many of their owners were well behind with payment. He said he wanted me to deal with it. I replied that in my opinion there were too many trucks on the depot ground anyway, and this was causing a major problem, due to our own vehicles not having sufficient room to park up safely when staff car parking was taken into consideration. He simply said, 'Well, sort it; I'll leave it entirely up to you.'

I contacted all the companies that owed us rent, and made it clear that they were in breach of the agreement signed by both parties, and that despite several requests (because Mike had told me this fact), they had not met their responsibilities, therefore the agreement was to be terminated and their vehicles must be removed at the earliest convenience.

I left the financial business to Mike, but I got rid of the vehicles – all of them, as a matter of fact. The days of the company renting out parts of Cannock Depot space to truck companies ceased forthwith... at least whilst I was the gaffer.

I didn't have or make many friends at Cannock, truth to tell. Apart from the people I've mentioned above, there was also Dave Grice; he is a really pleasant guy, and is still driving out of the old Cannock depot today (Cannock's work was split between D&G Bus and Coach Ltd, and Select Bus Services, during the spring/summer of 2021). Dave must have decided to stay at the former Cannock depot, because I am sure he would have been most welcome to join Select. So in deciding to stay at Cannock, Dave, amongst others, including Reg Mabberly – another nice guy – became an employee of D&G's Chaserider operations. Oddly, when I started with Midland Red North at Cannock back in the 1980s, our depot was called 'Chaserider'. Wellington had the title of 'Tellus'; Shrewsbury operated under 'Hotspur', and Tamworth ran out as 'Mercian'. Dave Grice became a friend, and is still a friend today. He even offered to clean my car a few times during my short tenure at Cannock; just a great bloke, and a top driver.

During the afternoon of 21st May 2001, my office telephone rang out: 'Hello, is that Alan Scriven?' a posh-sounding female voice asked. 'Yes,' I answered, thinking it was another manager's assistant, or more likely a member of Head Office staff.

'Hi. My name is Paula Cattermole, and I'm speaking to you from the Cabinet Office, at number ten Downing Street.'

I gave the poor woman a volley of good-natured verbal 'abuse', assuming someone from within the company was pulling my leg. She kindly allowed me to finish before saying, 'Mr Scriven, are you anywhere near a fax machine?'

'Yes,' I replied.

'Then please go to it now, and when you see the correspondence, please keep it to yourself, and return to me on the telephone.'

I sped off across the yard to Head Office, and looked at the fax machine; it was still spitting out its message, but I could clearly see the words: 'HONOURS SECTION, 10 DOWNING STREET' at the top! It was marked 'URGENT'. Moira, the receptionist, eyed me quizzically, and asked if everything was alright. 'Er, yes, Moira, no worries.' I ran back across to my office, and clumsily picked up the receiver. The first words I uttered to Ms Cattermole formed something of an apology for my initial outburst. She laughed and said not to worry as that kind of reaction was (quote) 'a regular occurrence'. The letter, signed by William Chapman, Secretary for Appointments read:

IN CONFIDENCE
Dear Sir

The Prime Minister has asked me to inform you, in strict confidence, that he has it in mind, on the occasion of the forthcoming Birthday Honours, to submit your name to The Queen with a recommendation that Her Majesty may be graciously pleased to approve that you be appointed a Member of the Order of the British Empire (MBE).

Before doing so, the Prime Minister would be glad to know that this would be agreeable to you. I should therefore be grateful if you would complete the enclosed form and send it to me by return of post.

If you agree, and The Queen accepts the Prime Minister's recommendation, the announcement will be made in the Birthday Honours List. You will receive no further communication before the List is published. Recipients will be notified within three months of the announcement.

I am, Sir
Your obedient Servant.

Wow! I was totally speechless. The good lady told me that if I agreed, then I must complete, sign and return the form which had been sent to my home, as a matter of urgency.

All I could say was: 'Why can't I tell anyone; how did you know where to find me?'

Her reply: 'If The Queen refuses, you'll look a fool, won't you? As for your second question... Mr Scriven, this is the Government!' Read into that statement what you will!

The form was actually waiting for me when I got home. I completed it, still in shock, and posted it on the following day, after I had taken it to show Tina and my boys... in confidence!

Her Majesty did accept the PM's recommendation, and correspondence of my appointment date at Buckingham Palace followed shortly after.

The award was given to me for my voluntary work with the Longmynd Adventure Camp. Amongst the first people to congratulate me were Neil Barker; Mr R. Taylor OBE, the Lord Lieutenant, and my former colleagues in the Traffic Office at Wellington. Neil even posted a staff notice informing everyone around the Arriva network of my award:

In the Queen's Birthday Honours List, announced on Saturday 16 June, Alan Scriven, PSM at Cannock was awarded an MBE for "Services to Disadvantaged Young People".

For many years Alan has given up his summer holidays to organise and run Summer Camps at Long Mynd for under-privileged children.

I am sure you will all join me in congratulating Alan in achieving this honour, in recognition of his commitment to others.

This was followed by a personal letter of congratulations from Neil, whom I had a conversation with on social media sometime in early March 2023, in which he kindly gave his permission for me to mention him in this book. Thank you, Neil.

A few days later, my home postman hand-delivered to me my 'Royal Warrant' signed (in blue/black ink) by HRH Prince Philip, Duke of Edinburgh (Grand Master), and Her Majesty Queen Elizabeth II.

Obviously, I treasure this document, which is framed and hangs in my living room (along with a couple of photographs of me with our now late Sovereign Lady). On 4th October 2001, I received a letter from Lieutenant Colonel Robert Cartwright, secretary of the Central Chancery of the Orders of Knighthood, informing me that my Investiture would take place on Thursday 6th December from 1100hrs, at Buckingham Palace.

Gail Travers, a friend from Wellington depot, kindly drove me, my sons Marc and Tom, and my sister Michelle to the palace. Gail knew London well, and I was very grateful for her kindness. She even took us on a sight-seeing trip after our four hours or so inside the palace. I couldn't have known it at the time, but Gail and I were destined to work together again, sooner than any of us imagined.

Just as an aside; people who have been decorated under the Order of the British Empire are entitled as are their children and grandchildren, to marry in the chapel of St Paul's Cathedral. I probably won't be taking our late Sovereign Lady up on that, however.

As we were having the official photographs taken within the palace grounds, the now late Prince Philip came round, driving a double-horse carriage; probably the same one which was paraded at his simple but well-planned funeral at Windsor Castle during the pandemic; and bequeathed to his granddaughter, Lady Louise Wessex. It was a great day; best of my life to date!

In the autumn of 2001, I was presented with a long service certificate. The citation read: *This Certificate for long and meritorious service has been presented to Alan Scriven MBE in recognition and appreciation of 15 years loyal and efficient service to the company.* It counted for absolutely nothing, however, just a short time later!

During February of 2002, I was summoned to John Morrow's office. Since May 2000, he had held the title of Operations Director. He sat me down and told me that Stuart Hyde (who was part of the second batch of drivers at Walsall, and someone I considered a friend) was leaving the company. He went on to say that Stuart had been successful in his application to join Telford and Wrekin Unitary Authority, as Mobility Manager, and would leave Arriva on 28th February. He was, at the time, Passenger Services Manager at Shrewsbury Depot.

Before I could respond with my congratulations for my colleague, Morrow stood up and walked around his desk to stand right beside me; maybe he thought it would give him a bit more authority... as if that was necessary!

Then in no uncertain terms, he told me that I was to replace Stuart at Shrewsbury.

I said, 'Thanks, but no thanks, John.'

He said: 'I'm not asking you, Scriv, I'm telling you!'

I tried my best to convince him that I was happy at Cannock; he sort of sneered at this, which immediately took my mind back to that conversation with Newcombe, which I had been promised would not hinder my current position with Arriva.

'You're going to apply for the Shrewsbury position as soon as it's posted, which will be in a couple of days at the outside.'

'And if I don't?'

'Let's just put it this way,' said Morrow, as he slowly returned to his side of the desk, 'you either apply for the job or you'll be out of the one you currently hold. I need to replace Stuart, and you are the best person for the job. I can get any one of half a dozen to do the Cannock job, but Shrewsbury needs a manager who knows the area.'

What a load of absolute, undiluted bullshit! I mean, they sent me to Cannock, didn't they? I didn't know that area from Outer Mongolia, and Stuart Hyde didn't know Shrewsbury when he took the job!

My experience of Shrewsbury was virtually nil, and I didn't want to go there; even after he attempted to sugar-coat his demand; saying he would give me an extra fifty pounds per month (until the end of the year – that statement proved pivotal when the end of the year actually arrived) to help with my travelling expenses, as I was now back living in Bushbury, Wolverhampton.

'Go away and consider my offer...'

I cut him short: 'Your fuckin' demand, you mean!'

'Whatever. I expect your application to arrive on this desk

immediately Stuart's leaving is made public knowledge.'

I walked out of his office. And as I descended the stairs of head office, I knew I was being faced with 'Hobson's Choice'... again!

I couldn't afford to lose my job, and I knew his threat was serious. I had, not many months earlier, sold my flat in Dawley and taken out another mortgage on a house in Bushbury, Wolverhampton. If he had said I was going back to (wonderful) Wellington, I would have been as happy as the proverbial pig in shit! Instead, however, I was in the shit, thanks to a pig!

A day or so following that debacle with Morrow, the company posted news of Stuart's departure. With it was an open invitation to apply for his position. I never actually put pen to paper, but after I came to the decision (all things considered) that I had no alternative but to go along with John's demand, the following was posted around the network:

STAFF CHANGES

Stuart Hyde, PSM for Shrewsbury has been successful in his application for the post of Mobility Manager with Telford and Wrekin Unitary Authority and leaves our company on 28 February 2002.

Consequently I am pleased to announce that Alan Scriven MBE, currently PSM at Cannock, who has vast previous experience of managing in the Shropshire area, will become PSM at Shrewsbury with effect from 1st March.

I am sure you will all join me in wishing Alan and Stuart the very best of luck in their new positions.

My final 'award' as Cannock boss was another certificate (they did love their certificates at Arriva) for: Achievement. I had completed yet another course on, ironically, 'Managing Conflict' on 15th February 2002. It was presented by Michelle Bartha, who at that time held the post of Training and Development Manager.

Chapter Eight

Shrewsbury:
The beginning of the end

'You cannot understand a city without using its Public transport system.' (Erol Ozan)

My short tenure at the 'Graveyard Depot' actually got off to a decent start. Just one month into my time there, I received a letter from Arriva's Head of Community and Public Affairs, Rebecca Wilson. She very kindly informed me that I had been successful in my application for a 'Community Action Award'. I had previously been invited by Neil Barker to apply for it because of my voluntary work with the Longmynd Adventure Camp. I was awarded £150, which was duly passed on to the LAC treasurer.

Then on 24th April, I was awarded yet another certificate, presented by Neil Barker, this time for 'Successfully Completing the Arriva Passenger Services Programme – DELIVERING A BETTER SERVICE'.

My office team at my final (as I thought at the time) Arriva depot consisted of Gail Travers (Staff Manager), whom I mentioned earlier, Dale Richards (Staff Supervisor), and a couple of duty clerks, including Colin Wood and the effervescent Arthur Williams. Arthur's initial words to me when I arrived on my first morning were: 'Can I call you Scriv? Welcome to the county town.' Brilliant! The final member of our team was Angie. She did a similar job to Carol Wallwork at Cannock. Angie, like Carol, was extremely capable, and I was glad to have her with us in the traffic office, where she had worked since long before I arrived.

I have to say that Dale was the best of the bunch. He did a great job, and in my eyes would have made a brilliant garage manager. Gail and Dale, as I have mentioned, were former Wellington colleagues of mine, so we all knew each other very well.

It soon became apparent, however, that I wasn't being very well received at Shrewsbury by the drivers, or the engineers. My office was upstairs, so maybe feelings of an 'us and him' syndrome prevailed; I don't know. Anyway, I didn't get much time to get to know the people, the depot, or the area, because on 5th September 2002 I was informed... by Morrow... quote: 'As a result of a review of current staffing levels and a reorganisation within Shropshire, your position as PSM Shrewsbury will be redundant.'

Read into that statement what you will!

I was further 'invited' to another meeting, on 12th September, during which, I was told, I would be provided with 'more details'.

There's no point in trying to sugar-coat this; I was being forced out! Things were never the same for me after what I said to Newcombe... or, oddly enough, after being awarded the MBE. One would have thought that the company would be proud of my achievement but if it was, it had a funny way of showing it! I never actually found out who put my name forward for the award; if it was anyone from the company, then the feeling that I was worth it obviously didn't last very long!

At that meeting, Morrow said I could apply for the vacant position of Area Manager North West, which meant, if successful, moving to Liverpool, because the job was based at Speke depot, apparently. To even my own surprise, I applied for the job... only to discover later (I was reliably informed) that no such position was on offer!

97

I wrote a very detailed letter of application, resulting in an invitation (from Morrow on 1st October) to attend Head Office for what turned out to be a 'smoke screen' interview. I even performed a presentation (not my strongest skill), but I was pissing in the wind anyway. It could have been the best presentation they had ever seen; it wouldn't have made a scrap of difference! Why I was put through this, I can't honestly say. Newcombe told me that I was the best of the applicants and it was obvious my experience in the industry had paid off. Bullshit!

A short while later, an incident of sorts occurred at my depot, which resulted in my withdrawal of interest in the vacancy that never existed!

We were very short of drivers at the time (this is an occurrence experienced at every depot at some time or other), mainly due to holidays and sickness. Gail, Dale and I had tried our level best to cover the duties for the coming Saturday (5th October), without success. I even asked Gail to speak to every other depot to ask for their spare drivers to come and work a duty for us. A negative response from everyone was the result, due (they told us) to having their own problems. This at least bears out my statement above, that all depots suffer staff shortages. Borrowing drivers from other depots was a common and accepted ploy to cover outstanding duties. But that agreement could only be implemented if drivers were available, and agreeable!

I myself took a bus out on the Tesco service, in an attempt to ease the burden for Gail and Dale. When I returned to the depot, however, I found Gail Travers in an obvious state of distress. She tearfully told me that the MD had spoken to Arthur Williams (why him, I don't know), saying that he was sending Mark Frost and Melvyn Westwood from Wellington depot to work on covering our outstanding duties. I hit the roof! Melvyn had been Staff Supervisor for me at Cannock until Morrow said a vacancy at Telford meant that either he or Brian Campbell would have to be transferred. I told him to have Mel, because I thought the move would help, in the fullness of time, to further his career, whereas Brian (being a little older) was happy to stay at his 'home' depot as my (then) Staff Manager.

Mel and 'Floss', both valued friends, arrived at the depot, with no magic wand. I told them, with gritted teeth, to carry on. They persuaded a couple of their own drivers to help us out, but they could have done that from Wellington, because Gail had asked them earlier. So it appeared to me that they were keen to show Mr Barker that they were capable of something I and my staff were not!

I was fuming; I had had enough! That was the final straw; the embarrassment it caused my staff and me was intolerable. My mind was made up... I probably played into Morrow's hands, but at the time I couldn't have cared less! Anyone who really knows me knows also that I speak my mind, and I am as straight as a gun barrel. So I wrote to Morrow, withdrawing all hitherto interest in the 'position' he had cajoled me into applying for, saying that as a result of the obvious slur on my staff, and my confidence and professionalism, I considered my application to be dead in the water! Reading through my employment records whilst writing this book, I found that there was apparently an A.M. position vacant, 'Area Manager West', which would cover Stafford and Cannock. I wasn't even considered for it.

The only response from my letter to Morrow was an invitation to continue the redundancy process at a meeting arranged for 28th October at Cannock. He pointed out that I had the right to union representation should I desire it... because, he told me, a redundancy situation is a form of dismissal. Well, I had enough past experience to be aware of that fact, prior to joining this crazy industry!

The situation dragged out until we were into the New Year. I had no clue as to where I stood. My most recent discussion with Morrow had led me to believe that there was still a place for me within the company. He mentioned the A.M. vacancy, as noted above, but also asked me to consider a Traffic Manager position at Shrewsbury or Telford, although adding (quote): 'I have my eye on someone for that post.' Unbelievable, you might think, that he actually said that... but he did! If that wasn't a smack in the mouth, I don't know what it was!

I declined his disrespectful and derogatory 'offers' there and then. And, with the fullness of time, I am glad that I did.

It all came to a dramatic climax on 7th January 2003, when I wrote to John Morrow after leaving the company. Here are some excerpts from my 'no punches pulled' letter:

Dear Mr Morrow

Following yours and the H.R. Manager's decision that I was unsuccessful in my bid for one of the two A.M. positions within Arriva Midlands North (one of which you wrongly said existed, and were open for application), I have taken some time to consider my current situation.

Of the six internal applicants (which made a total of eighteen) I was the most senior at the time the initial interviews took place on 18/12/02. I was very surprised therefore that not only was I not invited back for a second interview; I wasn't even debriefed following my first, which Mr Newcombe, one of the interviewing panel, said had gone 'very well'. He also added (quote): "It was obvious from the presentations performed, who was actually involved in the industry." With that in mind I was quietly confident that I would be successful, at least in getting a second interview...

To add insult to injury, I received a TEXT MESSAGE from (HRM), whilst I was on holiday, asking me to present myself at H.O. to see her, and yourself at 1000hrs on Thursday 02 January 2003; no reason given however, so on that basis I obviously and quite naturally expected to be offered the position (despite our recent altercations). That is the reason I arrived without union representation.

You opened the discussion by asking if I wanted

representation, but even then I did not see why I should need it. After all, I had received a text message not a formal letter (as on all previous occasions throughout this abysmal process).

You then stated quite simply, and coldly, that I had been unsuccessful, and my position as PSM Shrewsbury was redundant from 31 Dec' 2002. You added that I had refused to consider the two Traffic Manager vacancies. I told you why I had refused, but I'll repeat it here: It was demotion, and I couldn't understand why you would want to embarrass me by my applying for demotion rather than promotion!

I had served the company for sixteen years. I had a clean conduct, and attendance record. At no time was I ever advised either formally or informally by any of my superiors that I had acted unprofessionally in any way. That of course excludes the quite ridiculous comments you made whilst I was PSM at Cannock, and then later at my first redundancy consultation at Shrewsbury, saying I was "uncommunicative". As well; at that meeting you made the absurd remark that I "insisted that the drivers wore their uniform correctly." I mean, John, I ask you...really?! If that wasn't looking for confrontation I'll sleep out...

The fact is that I have always carried out my responsibilities in every position I have ever held, in as professional a manner as I possibly could. But it's easy I suppose for you, and people like you, to make such degrading comments, even with your vast depot experience and knowledge of how people can behave sometimes. I repeat however, that I had never been advised that I was performing my duties below the standard of what was required, and expected of me...

May I remind you that during the last few weeks of my time at Shrewsbury, I was without my staff manager, and staff supervisor. Yet I still managed to significantly increase the driving staff, and reduce lost mileage etc., as well as run the depot alone! Mr Newcombe congratulated me, and even said that my efforts and work-rate had been noticed by head office...yeh right...Bullshit!

Without the opportunity of a debrief after my interview and presentation etc, I am at a loss as to why I was deemed unfit for the A.M. position; you know, the one that actually existed. But being honest with myself, I knew deep down that I wouldn't succeed; the odds were stacked against me even before I was forced to go to Shrewsbury, weren't they John (it's not a question).

Do you remember calling me up to your office on Monday 11th February 02, when I was PSM at Cannock?

You told me that Stuart Hyde's job was to become vacant, and that I should go away; think about it...then return to your office and beg: "please John may I have Stuart's job". You told me as well, that if I didn't take it, I would effectively be out!

It was 'Hobson's Choice' wasn't it John? A very thinly veiled threat actually!

I can be so precise regarding dates etc because I recorded every detail in my day-book (a practice I have been committed to since joining the company), which cannot possibly be disputed!

On Thursday 12th February my day-book records that Mr Newcombe came into my office and said that he had "just heard the news" about me going to Shrewsbury. He told me not to say anything to anyone. Well how could I when the all important staff notice hadn't been posted, had it? And more importantly, I hadn't as yet dutifully returned to your office to continue the farce, as directed...by you!

I don't doubt for one second that you had put Mr Newcombe in the picture, after all, he's your faithful servant isn't he, chosen ahead of Kevin Walker for some strange reason...

On the morning of Wednesday 13th February my day-book records that I had a chat with Eddie Owen (Stafford PSM). He asked me if I knew anything about the managerial positions. I replied that I expected to go to Shrewsbury. He replied 'that's not fair; I wanted Shrewsbury.' Then I had to think fast, adding that I had told you that I wouldn't mind going to Shrewsbury! Yes John; I was that scared of losing my job!

Eddie Owen said he thought something 'was happening today.' What insight! It is my belief that Eddie was well aware of what was actually happening!

I dutifully reported to you, as instructed, and continued the "game". But it was totally and absolutely against my will, and you knew it John; you bloody well knew it.

As a "softener" you said you would give me an extra £50 per month until Dec' 02, which, incidentally aligned with my redundancy date, (but I reckon, given everything that has occurred, that you knew that anyway) to cover fuel expenses; how very considerate of you!!

My day-book further reveals that on Thursday 14th Feb 02 I received a call from Gail Travers (the then Shrewsbury Staff Manager). She asked if it was true that I was coming to Shrewsbury as PSM. She added that you had told her during the previous day. But I had yet to continue the farce by agreeing to your demands... talk about a 'conspiracy'!

Another indication that my current plight had been pre-empted came when I read an email from Michelle Bartha. It stated that various (named) personnel from all depots were to attend a meeting at Head Office. My name was not included...

Obviously I have thought long and hard about what I must have done to fall foul of you and Anica Goodwin; a couple of things spring to mind: My telling Mr Newcombe (at my previous appraisal in 2001) that it would be nice if H.O. personnel refrained from interfering with the day to day operation of Cannock depot. Mr Newcombe told me that he understood, appreciated, and accepted my concerns; he even agreed with them! He said he would take my comments back to H.O. and tell them, even the directors, which I didn't think was necessary. After that appraisal yours (and others) attitude changed towards me. You accused me of that "old chestnut" of being uncommunicative with the drivers, as you had done *previously to Peter Ralphs. I can't speak for Peter, but it was a ridiculous accusation to make against me... and you know it! It's an important pre-requisite of my job to be communicative; you've known me from day one John. How could you be so hurtfully ridiculous? ...*

So, in answer to your "invitation" to sign a "compromise agreement" for "blood money" at that cold consultation, I don't think I will; thank you very much...!

I feel strongly after considering everything that the company (YOU and her, of late) has put me through, that I have been treated most unfairly, and unprofessionally. I will not therefore even consider your derisory offer to pay the tax and N.I. of my notice period; blood money as I said above!

I have been deprived unfairly, of my employment; my final salary pension and all of its benefits, along with everything else appertaining to the terms and conditions of my employment contract. I have given this company the best years of my working life to date, and in return, the company has disregarded me, and abandoned me in 'spectacular fashion'. And I obviously don't mean that as a compliment...

Not to mention the acute embarrassment and humiliation you have so unnecessarily caused me. I wasn't even given the opportunity to say farewell to my colleagues at Shrewsbury, or anywhere else for that matter...

I am told that the current situation regarding the Shropshire A.M. position is at the 'second interview' stage. But as I say above, and repeat now, I wasn't asked back for a second interview despite performing well (as both yourself, and Mr Newcombe conceded) at my initial interview. I was a PSM, a Garage Manager with a totally clean conduct record after sixteen years' service...and as your Staff Notice pointed out, regarding the PSM position at Shrewsbury you forced on me: 'very experienced in Shropshire'. And yet I wasn't even considered for the position. Shame on you, and your cronies... You shit on me John, twice!

I am hoping that my advisors will agree that I have been 'constructively dismissed'. But if not, then at least I can say that I maintained my dignity by refusing your attempt to silence me with "blood money", in the form of that so called 'offer' you made to me earlier on during your despicable attitude and behaviour!
Happy New Year!
Alan Scriven MBE

Even though I was advised that I had a 'good case' for constructive dismissal, at the hands of 'double-dyed' Morrow and his side-kick Goodwin, I decided not to pursue it because to be honest, I felt sick to my stomach with the whole affair; and my sister Pat was now very ill, and I didn't need to spend my time worrying about any other situation but hers.[5]

As it turned out, shortly after commencing employment with Choice Travel, I was offered a return to Arriva in a managerial position. I politely refused!

And as if to lighten this dark episode of my working career, a while later, both Morrow and Newcombe "left" the company.

Ah well, what goes around...

I was glad, actually; once I had cleared my mind of the hurt those bastards had inflicted on me, to be no longer a part of Arriva Midlands North Ltd. However, if I thought the company was out of my hair for good, I was in for a very rude awakening a little further down the line!

---

[5] *My sister passed away on 19th February 2003.*

'Just passed our tests'. Ken Parker, me and Dave Fryer' Dec 1986.

Midland Red North football squad, early 90s: Front L, Dave Wilde; me, front 3rd
left; Simon Gray-Davis (goalkeeper), and Colin Turner, referee.

A very young Ian Tully (early 90s)

On the 'Wackies'

Receiving my NVQ certificate from Arriva director Mike Doyle.

Being presented with the MBE from The Queen, 2001.

A retirement bus pull. The driver was Ken Gough. With L. Brian Campbell, John Morrow, and Clive Bevington.

Claire Wilde and me at Select Bus Services.

Chapter Nine

A Wise 'Choice'

Immediately following that ambush by Morrow and Goodwin, which culminated in them making a point of telling me that I could appeal their decision, after saying that I was now no longer an employee of the company, I drove to Shrewsbury depot. I said above that I wasn't given the opportunity to bid farewell to my staff, or anyone else around the depot, so one might consider this to be a false statement because of the fact that I went back to my (former) depot. But the truth is that as I got out of my car, Nick Newcombe pounced on me, asking why I was there. 'Oh, so you know then, Nick, that I've been sacked' – well I had, effectively, and for no fair or obvious reason.

He actually had the brass face to deny all knowledge of their decision at H.O. Three questions arise, however, if that was indeed the case:

    a)   Why was he (obviously) waiting for my arrival?

    b)   How come he had gathered all my personal belongings from my office, so that I had no reason to enter it?

    c)   Why was no member of my former staff anywhere to be seen?

As I mentioned earlier, I wasn't even afforded the decency of being allowed to speak to anyone at Shrewsbury Depot on my last ever day there. What a nasty and diabolical way to treat someone who had given the company the service that I had over the previous sixteen years or so.

It seemed that my comments regarding Head Office staff constantly interfering with the day-to-day business of Cannock Depot, coupled with not jumping at the chance to manage the so-called 'graveyard depot', had effectively sealed my fate!

Having worked for the company since its halcyon days as Midland Red, I received the redundancy payment due to me. In hindsight, I should have invested the pay-out, but all I did was take nearly six months out, before realising I had to find another job. Did I even want to stay in this crazy industry?

At this point, I would like to offer my apologies to those that weren't in the know, for giving a false reason for leaving Arriva in 2003. I told people that I left because senior management wanted to move us depot managers around yet again; reduce our salary, and expect us to agree, and to be honest, there was some truth in that. The reason I came up with this explanation for leaving, however, was out of pure embarrassment that my abilities in the industry had been so severely and horribly cast aside, for (obviously) daring to speak against the will of Head Office! Of course, my take on issues can be disputed by any of the people who were involved, but my opinion will never change.

As I was now living in Wolverhampton again, I needed to find something relatively local. I didn't fancy West Midlands Travel (National Express these days) after applying, and taking a successful 'driving test' with them (I was asked to drive a double-decker from the depot in Park Lane, Low Hill to a former service no.3 turn-around at the top of Bushbury Hill, and back).

And having been informed that I had passed the driving test, I was invited to join the company, but in the end I decided against it. I had never really fancied working for such a seemingly over regimented company; more so than Arriva... apparently!

So instead I looked at Liyell Limited, which traded as 'Choice Travel'; a small company located in Planetary Road, Wednesfield. I rang its owner, Mr Tom Young, enquiring if any vacancies existed. He knew me, so stated immediately that no managerial positions were available, but he was looking for a suitable person to train new drivers. I said I would consider it and get back to him. I wrote to him on 9th June 2003, saying that I didn't fancy the 'driver-trainer' position but would be happy just to drive. I received the following a few days later:

Dear Mr Scriven
Thank you for your letter dated 09/06/2003.
Since receiving it we have tried several times to contact you, with no success.
Could you therefore ring us – or better still pop in to see us.
We have a Driver vacancy at the present time, and you would be most welcome to join us.
Yours Sincerely
Mr T D Young
Director.

I contacted Mr Young (he said, 'Call me Tom,' because as I said above, I knew of him from my time with Arriva) and I began working for him, as a driver (which actually was all I wanted) on 24th June 2003. I was determined never again to accept a management position in this crazy industry, but that was to change (at least for a period) after D&G Bus and Coach, owned by David Reeves and Gerald Henderson (both now lost to us) purchased Choice Travel from Tom Young on 22nd April 2005.

My new employment meant a considerable drop in wages, but I was very happy with my lot. Just to get away from Arriva was well worth it!

I settled in at Choice, making a few new friends, including Martin Barratt, Tony Brunyee, Andy Stirrup, Kalvinder Singh and his son Charanjit Sandhu, Phil Pidgeon, Adrian Lloyd, Colin

Shaw, Surinder Grewal, Sucha Sergill, Kulvinder Singh and in due course William Bryant, Simon and Rob Harris, Chris Dell, Martin Clarke, Nick Gough, Rob Taylor, Paul Davis, Rob Lowe (Engineering Manager), Mick Bowen and many others, which included in the fullness of time (when we were joined at Wednesfield by some drivers from Hill Top depot) Geoff Green, Adam French and Dean and Steve Cooksey. Mick Bowen became a good friend, and it was very sad to hear from his granddaughter Sharne Robinson that he had passed away from Covid-19. Sharne kindly invited me to the funeral, but owing to limited numbers being allowed to attend due to the pandemic, I wasn't able to.

Rob Lowe and I got on well too, becoming friends almost immediately. Rob knew his stuff, but for some reason it wasn't good enough for those making the top decisions, so Rob opted for a change of scenery, putting his skills to work for TWM (National Express today).

When D&G purchased Choice Travel from Tom Young and his wife Sarah, they kept our depot as Choice Travel for a while, but we were very much under the umbrella of the new owners. I linked up with Dave Wilde again in 2003; we were both a part of the Midland Red football team back in the 1990s, when he was based at Cannock. Dave was to become Garage Manager at Wednesfield, and in the fullness of time, I became his joint assistant... for six months only, by my own choice.

One year after we came under the D&G 'banner', a company newsletter was inaugurated under the title of D&G and Choice Travel. The directors wrote a piece on the front page, telling us that this idea was born out of a necessity to keep in touch with the workforce. It lasted for just the one edition, I believe I'm right in saying...well, I only have that first issue, and I keep everything!

For the benefit of any former Wednesfield staff, here is the report as it was published in the newsletter:

News from Choice Travel

April 22nd saw the acquisition of Choice Travel to the D&G fold. The business was made up of a mixture of bus and coach work with some coach excursions together with a loyal team of employees. Dave and I found the bus side of the business ran on a similar basis to the D&G manner, with reliable drivers who are able to communicate with their passengers on a friendly basis. The fleet, made up of a mixture of Mercedes, Optare Solo's and Dennis Darts totalled 37.

As the year progressed we looked at the way we wanted to structure the business for future development, this meant various changes on both the engineering and the managing side.

Meanwhile success in the tendering market with Worcestershire County Council was gained, operating services in the Kidderminster, Bewdley and Stourport areas. For this operation 'Super Low Floor' vehicles were purchased. At the same time two of D&G's vehicles, 16 and 17 were moved to the Wolverhampton based depot.

In October 2005 Centro work was won; this again has resulted in the purchase of two Wright bodied Dennis Dart, plus six SLF's. This brought us up to the Christmas period and the 'dark nights in the Black Country', many thanks to the staff that worked over the Christmas and New Year period.

The New Year has seen changes in the office lay-out. In the main building offices were refurbished for the Traffic Office Supervisors, and Traffic Manager, leaving the portakabin as a rest-room for the drivers, cleaners and engineering staff.

I would like to thank all the staff during the early stages of this transitional period for their patience and understanding.

Gerald Henderson, Operations Director.

Sadly, Gerald passed away, very suddenly and not long after the purchase, so he never saw the company's progression.

As well as Gerald's report, the magazine included a 'Welcome to our New Colleagues' piece:

A big welcome to all new employees; including Gareth Woodhouse (Traffic Manager), who joined us in February.

Drivers: Harry Atwell, Bernard Bennion, Hugh Carmody, Chris Dell, Surinder Harra, Robert Hitchin, Mark Hulme, Russell Jones, Peter King, Chris Nock, Lee Ryall, Jeffrey Salmon, Kehar Singh, Bikar Singh and Michelle White.

Garage: Steve Andrews.

Congratulations to Nanette Johnson and Neil Snook who were promoted to Traffic Office Supervisors in January, and Phil Allen and Steve Corr who were also promoted to Engineering Manager, and Garage Supervisor respectively.

Congratulations also to the following drivers who have completed their NVQ in Road Passenger Transport; Chris Dell, Alan Scriven, Russell Jones and Bernard Bennion.

To the reader, seeing my name as a driver, and completing a NVQ course requirement, it might appear that I was back where I started in 1986. And to a certain degree, he/she would be correct. But after leaving Arriva in such poor circumstances, I had no interest whatsoever in entering into management again, and I was happy to undergo any and all courses offered. David Reeves, however, had other ideas; more about this later.

On 1st May 2006, we all received notice that our Contract of Employment was to change. We were, however, reassured that this was only intended to 'tidy up existing contracts and ensure that all members of staff have had a contract issued'.

The correspondence also included a copy of the individual agreement to opt out of the 48-hour maximum average working week. I didn't take up this offer!

In the summer of 2006, I was elected – by my peers – a member of the so-called 'Works Committee' (representing the drivers). Other members included Dave Wilde and Neil Snook for the Traffic Office, and Phil Allen, on behalf of the Engineers. Management was represented by Dave Reeves and Paul Loughead.

The purpose of the committee was to 'provide a regular forum for Drivers and Staff at Choice Travel to discuss with local and senior management any issues relating to working relationships'. It added that, where possible, normal channels of discussion should be conducted locally. The committee met bi-monthly.

A bonus scheme was introduced, offering a maximum of £120.00 for any driver who remained free of blameworthy accidents for twelve months. And on 23rd November 2006, I received notice that I would be paid the maximum amount on 01/12/06. Insurance costs at this point in time were, according to Mr Reeves, costing the company in the region of £500,000 per annum.

In 2007, the bonus had increased to £150.00, and again I qualified for the total pay-out. By this time, Dave Wilde had become Garage Manager.

In December of that year, the Works Committee increased in number, due mainly to more drivers being employed; a large number being Polish. Joining me were W. Bury, K. Vernon, H. Mierzjewski and K. Singh.

The Polish drivers and cleaning staff were all very decent and likeable folk, and I rubbed along soundly with most of them.

One morning, however, as I sat in my bus preparing myself for my departure from the depot, Kristof, a Polish driver with a very short fuse (like me) came to me and in an irate manner told me to shift my bus out of his way. I tried explaining that I would be ready to go in a minute or two, but this only inflamed a growing blow-up! He stormed off in the direction of the box (near the gate) where the free Metro newspapers were kept. We were all asked to take some papers with us, so I decided to get some, too. Fortunately, or not, Claire Wilde (who was by this time part of the office team) was also on the yard. Kristof was coming towards me, obviously still very angry, and a blazing row began as we stood toe to toe! He wasn't backing down, and I most definitely wasn't. As the situation escalated to the point of, let's just say a gross misconduct charge, Claire quickly stepped in between us.

'Get out of my way, Claire,' I said with gritted teeth, 'I'm gonna sort this twat once and for all.'

She looked up at me and said, 'You'll have to hit me first, now go back to your bus.' Kristof had begun to back away, but I was seething. 'Move, Claire,' I said. 'No way,' she replied. I asked her again; she stood her ground and repeated her absolute refusal. 'Gonna hit me, Scriv, cus I'm not moving?'

I realised I was in a no-win situation. We were best friends, and here she was, standing between me and certain dismissal, because the mood I was now in caused me to think of nothing other than violence. I stepped back, turned around, and headed back to my bus.

She had no alternative but to report the incident, because it had been witnessed by other drivers. Raj Chumber, the Garage Manager, decided that if neither I nor Kristof made an official complaint, the matter was resolved with no further action. And that was how it panned out in the end. So I had Claire to thank for taking the decision to enter the fray... which she later told me scared the crap out of her!

Four months earlier, I had been promoted to Inspector, along with Mac Morris, Rob Harris, and Claire Wilde. Claire suggested to Dave Wilde (her then partner) that we two should work together, at least initially, to give her some confidence should the grim task of having to report a driver arose. Dave agreed, and this arrangement worked brilliantly, though not always to the standard probably expected of us, if truth be told...

Working together since 2003, we became friends, as we still are to this day; in fact, at the time of writing, we are back working together again.

On our first day out doing the job of checking that our services were operating as efficiently as possible, we succeeded in losing all of our official paperwork, to a very gusty wind! This caused great mirth between us, making us realise that we could perhaps have some fun, as well as do what we were being paid for; the fun aspect, however, overtook the 'official requirement' somewhat.

After our initial attitude of 'Come on, let's do a great job together', we sort of, well, relaxed, if you will. It started with me kicking a stone along a pavement in or around Bloxwich, if memory serves. I was ahead of Claire, so decided to 'back heel' the stone to her, then turning, I challenged her to kick it past me; she succeeded, so we decided to have a game of who could score the most 'goals' against the other. And you know... despite my recognised football ability (no comment, Simon Gray-Davis and Dave Wilde, please), I never once beat Claire! From this, we progressed to buying a regular-size leather football (Claire possibly paid), which we took to various parks – and even a motorway services car park once – to enjoy a kick-about, whilst our buses went sailing past, oblivious to what we were up to! And on most days, we would sample the chippie in whichever area we happened to be, or were supposed to be 'checking'; terrific fun.

At the end of each 'working day', half of which we might have spent in the traffic office for some concocted reason, we filled out an Inspector's Report Form, lying through our teeth on what we had supposedly done to benefit the greater good of the depot. We *did* do *some* inspecting... just not a lot!

Spending time working together during the day (well, as I say above, we actually did work, sometimes) and some evenings too led to us spending the occasional evening out together, socially. We made no secret of our friendship (which is all it has ever been) but as people are prone to do, some people thought there was more to it. However, Claire's partner Dave was happy (as far as I know) with us being friends. On those evenings out, all we ever did was either drive to Marston Green in Birmingham and watch the aeroplanes taking off, or landing, depending on the wind direction; or just drive around till we invariably got ourselves lost! Somehow, though, we always found ourselves opposite West Bromwich Albion Football Stadium, at McDonald's (Claire probably paid), where we had a cup of drinking chocolate; or a meal at Burger King somewhere (Claire definitely paid).

On our social evenings, Claire on most occasions had some shopping to do, so we would visit large stores. And on every occasion, I would find something to make Claire laugh...and sometimes even embarrass her, but she loved it really! In one of the big stores that sold everything, we came across a single bed, made up and ready to sleep in. I wasted no time in pulling the quilt back and sliding under it, with my boots on; great fun.

It was not to last, however, because I was asked by Dave Reeves to apply for a new office vacancy (Operations Assistant), which he said would be posted towards the end of September 2008. He told me he had reviewed my CV and felt that it would be a good move for the company, and indeed me, if I fancied it. I have to say that my initial response was negative. I explained to Dave that I was happy doing what I was doing. He said he accepted my reply... or did he?

Some short while later, I was at the depot when Mr Reeves arrived. He parked his car across the road where the buses were kept, then rang the office and asked for me to come over to him. He had done his homework, to know that I would be on a break at the depot at the time of his arrival. When I got to his car, I saw Mr Julian Peddle sitting quietly in the passenger seat. I walked round to Dave's side. He lowered the window and said: 'Hi Alan, you know Julian, don't you?'

'Yes, Dave. Hi Julian,' I said. He looked my way fleetingly, then nodded. 'Look, Alan,' Dave continued, 'I want you in the office, and preferably as manager.'

Wow! Where did that come from?

I told Dave in no uncertain terms that there was no way I was pulling the carpet from under Dave Wilde. I said that Dave was a good friend and had been since a long time ago, and I would not under any circumstances take his position, whatever it meant for me. In point of fact, when I first joined Choice, a lot of people, including the Wilde couple, assumed I had been headhunted to take the manager's position. Nothing could have been further from the truth, as I had assured Claire when she accompanied me as a guide on an evening run in Willenhall, just after I joined the company.

Dave Reeves came back with a compromise... of sorts: 'Look mate, I like Dave (Wilde), he's good at certain aspects of his job... but he's not strong enough. He needs a 'father figure', if you will. And if you agree to do the Operations Assistant job, it will bear fruit, but I give you my word; I will not replace Dave with you... if that's what you want.'

Julian looked at me in a kind of quizzical manner but said nothing.

'The position will be advertised. You apply, and we'll take it from there.'

'OK, Dave. I'm grateful for the confidence you have in me, and I'll work with Dave, we get along great.'

'Right, that's that then, thank you, Scriv. I know that's what you prefer to be called.' He had done his homework!

And so it transpired; the vacancy was posted – but as a three-month temporary position – stating that the job could be made permanent for the right candidate. I applied, as requested, on 23rd September, after reassuring Claire Wilde that I had no intention of taking Dave's job.

An interview was arranged for Tuesday 7th October at 1500 hrs. The interviewing panel consisted of Dave Reeves and Dave Wilde. Naturally, I sailed through the proceedings and on 9th October, the following was posted on the notice board:

I signed a new contract of employment on 13th October 2008.

At my first Traffic Office meeting, on Tuesday 21st October, along with Dave Reeves, Dave Wilde and our Fleet Engineer Gary Burgoyne, my report focused on Inspector usage as well as my Ops Assistant duties.

I liked Gary Burgoyne; he was a good bloke who liked a joke, but knew his job. The company purchased some Solo Optare buses, and Claire Wilde and I went to Rotherham with Gary on a couple of occasions, to drive them back to Wednesfield. I'm not sure what happened between Dave Reeves and Gary; they appeared to be great friends, but surprisingly, Gary left the company sometime later.

If I remember correctly, it was about this time that the company introduced the 'Green Road System', and what a pain in the arse that ridiculous idea was! Each bus was fitted with a horizontal panel of tiny lights in the colours of traffic lights, but beginning with green, then a couple of ambers, before a few red ones. They were positioned on the dash, behind the steering wheel, right in view of the driver, whenever you looked below the windscreen. There was also a little button-type-thing that you had to touch with another small contraption which hung on a lanyard around your neck. This was to identify you to the office as the driver of that bus until you 'signed off'. The concept of the Green Road System was to teach professional drivers how to drive professionally; yes, what a farcical waste of money. It was so sensitive that there was no way of keeping out of the red lights on a regular basis... and your performance was signalled and conveyed to the spies in the traffic office. So you either got a letter pointing out your unacceptable performance; or you received a certificate of competence if you were amongst the 'top drivers'. And if you did take it seriously (not many did), you would find yourself running up to twenty minutes late, in order to stay out of the red lights. Ridiculous! It was dispensed with, eventually, to I'm sure one hundred per cent approval from the drivers.

I posted a notice on 5th November regarding my 'developing a working rota for members of the traffic office supervisors'. The notice included Neil Snook. Neil actually became Assistant Manager to Dave... as I did too, a little later. My upgrade came about when Dave Reeves suggested I stay as an office member after my three-month stint as Ops Assistant ended. So this is what Dave Reeves meant when he initially spoke to me about joining Dave Wilde in the office. I didn't have a problem with Neil, but his body language whenever we were in close proximity to each other suggested, in my mind anyway, that he didn't like me much. On the surface, we got along, but I always suspected that he thought I was hell-bent on replacing him. The fact is, however, that when Dave Reeves said I would be Dave Wilde's assistant, he also said he 'had plans' for Neil. I just thought he would move into another position. As things turned out, it was me who left the office, following another altercation with a 'superior' (more on this later).

Claire Wilde had made terrific progress in the industry, since initially starting her career as a cleaner at Choice Travel (Wednesfield depot), at the young age of sixteen years. And she would go on to yet greater success in the fullness of time, with Arriva, and Select Bus Services. Claire currently holds a Certificate of Professional Competence (CPC), which should guarantee her employment with any company she chooses. That said, she wouldn't *need* the qualification to find alternative employment should she feel the need to move on... from wherever.

During my time as a Passenger Services Manager (Garage Manager) with Arriva, I was asked to take a CPC at my own expense; I politely refused, saying the company should meet the cost. That response may have further assisted the senior management in making their decision to dispense with my services in 2003... albeit by the 'back door'.

I was still doing a certain amount of driving (when required) whilst performing my office duties, and on 25th November I received confirmation that I had again qualified for the full Accident Bonus of £150.00. The reader might assume that it would be easy for an office person to achieve the full bonus amount, due to doing less driving, but one still had to drive without being involved in a blameworthy accident, plus, Dave Reeves paid out on an average of hours worked; I had worked an average of 51+ hours per week that year, as his letter to me with regard to my bonus stated!

As 2008 rolled on towards Christmas, I was asked to present another appraisal of the Inspectors. My report included a list of the duties our Inspectors were expected to undertake:

- Check that all passengers have the correct ticket or pass; reporting all 'irregularities'.
- Check that the ticket machine is operating correctly.
- Ensure defecting procedure has been followed.
- Identify any obvious reasons for attracting negative

Centro reports i.e. incorrect destination; early/late running; incorrect bus station procedure (being on wrong stand; speeding, abandoned buses); late, or missed journeys.

- Assist drivers with any day-to-day problems they may experience.

Whilst I do feel that the use of a Mystery Shopper has its benefits, none of the above could be performed by them, due to having to protect their anonymity.

And our Inspectors <u>have</u> produced results!

Tim Jeffcoat, whom I knew from our Arriva days, had decided (apparently) from D&G Headquarters in Longton, Stoke-on-Trent, to cancel inspectors' mileage allowances, so as a result they ceased using their own vehicles, resorting to public transport, and not always ours, so would on occasions present an expenses claim with their fare tickets as proof. Since they have been working to Tim Jeffcoat's lay-out, the inspectors have not been used to their full potential, mainly due to missed connections as a result of services not operating, or early/late running. Incidentally, I made Simon Harris an inspector when I joined the traffic office team.

Mentioning early/late operation of services reminds me that Arriva employed (from within) a 'Reliability Monitor'. It was his/her responsibility to report any discrepancies to the official timetable. One monitor was sitting in his van, eyeing proceedings at Gaol Square bus station in Stafford through a pair of binoculars! Unfortunately for him, Gordon Brannan (at that time a driver at Stafford depot) clocked his apparent 'suspicious behaviour', and promptly called the police!

The following is by no means an attempt to show one of our Polish drivers in a bad or negative light, but I couldn't resist sharing it with my readers. It is a driver's letter of appeal following a dismissal award for a serious accident. I will protect the identity of the driver, and withhold the date. I sincerely hope, if he reads this book, that he does not take offence, because none is intended. I just thought it would add to the book's light-hearted moments. Below is exactly as it was written:

<u>To the Management of Choice Travel</u>
I turn with the dismissal / the request to the management in the relationship with the situation which she had the place in the day and undertaken decision by the management of the firm about the solution in the day... the contract about works.

I turn from the request about the renewed party me on the tentative period. I solved in the Poland my contract about works because of low earnings. She was the direct reason of my arrival to Great Britain the necessity earns on serious the operations surgical to my fiancée.

I earned all money which they became he pushes from me sent to the Poland. The fiancée spends from ten days in the hospital and I will need the centres on her more far treatments and rehabilitations very much. He depends on me this work very much.

I was engaged in Choice Travel by this period when I gave to become acquainted as the conscientious worker situation which had the place in the day...

I lesson which will remember on the future and draw out suitable conclusions.

I ask for the dish me the last chance on show from I am the good worker and I assure from I will make all so that such situation oneself more does not repeat any more.

And he obliges himself in the measure of the modest my possibilities to the turn of the costs of the repair of the bus.

Bless him; he obviously had some personal stuff going on which I can't now recall. I have the copy of his appeal letter, so I may have played a part in the award decision, although my memory of it has faded somewhat.

In light-hearted continuation, the following letter was sent to me (or so I thought at the time) in 2009 by a Russian girl whom I had supposedly met whilst on holiday in Prague with Ian Tully.

I later discovered that my so-called work mates had tried to set me up, as it were, after I had told them a little something about what Ian Tully and I had got up to in the Czech Republic city of Prague:

Hello Mr Alan Scriv

I am Natalie, Russian girl-lady who long time is loving you. The Bulgaria men they say unto me it is the hot sex they are wanting, but I know that Alan is my lovely and that sex he not want. My soul it sings in the house of my grandmother who has 147 years of old. I think many times every night of you and your wallet and I am much longing for your passport and you spend big money on me. The men of Bulgaria they do not understand but my mother dearest know that my Alan love is big, and he understands me long time. I count the days until the airline ticket she arrive in my box, and we can together forever be.

Much and many love
Natalia xx

The 'letter' was accompanied by a photograph of a girl with the face that only a mother could love!

Chapter Ten

Back on the road again

By 2009, we had a new General Manager at Wednesfield depot; his name was Steve Elms. I hadn't come across him, or indeed heard of him, during my previous years in this crazy industry. He was a most likeable chap, was Steve, and I, and I'm sure Dave Wilde (who remained as Garage Manager – for a while) and the rest of the office team got along with him really well. Steve, if memory serves, had been put in position by our new operations director; a man called Shaz Ali. Now, whether or not Dave Reeves had told Shaz of his earlier, failed attempt to replace DW with me, I don't know, but Mr Ali made it his business to try and succeed where the MD had failed. I can't tell you the number of occasions that he told me at every opportunity: 'You will be the next garage manager here, and very soon, too.' And on every single occasion, I repeated what I had said to Mr Reeves (in the presence of Mr Peddle): I had absolutely no interest in replacing my friend Dave Wilde, and I was happy and content doing what I was being paid to do, as a member of Dave's traffic office team. But he insisted; to no avail!

The result was that Shaz tried to make life as difficult as he could for all of us! He became terrible to work with, and for. But I resolved that he wouldn't brow-beat me, even if some of the others shit themselves (metaphorically speaking of course) whenever Mr Ali was in the vicinity.

Situations, however, have a way of working out. Over the Easter period of 2009, that's exactly what happened for me. But prior to that, on 20th March, Steve Elms wrote to me (and every other office member), saying that he had been reviewing the performance of the traffic office, and his opinion was that it was overstaffed, which was creating 'operational and economic inefficiencies'. He went on to say that the coming weeks would bring in fewer contracts, leading to a reduction of duties, the number of vehicles required, and hours of coverage. It was clear, he added, that this situation had to be addressed.

A meeting was arranged for Wednesday 25th March, to discuss proposals for the way forward. Well, it didn't need a very intelligent person to deduce that some of us would be kicked out of the office. But bearing in mind Shaz Ali's constant threat to replace Dave Wilde with me, I considered that I was as safe as I wanted to be, in there, because if they got rid of me, his plans were dead in the water. That said, I had tired of being back in a traffic office environment, and had been looking for a way out for a while. I saw this as an opportunity to get back behind the wheel, on my 341/342 duty that had been agreed when I initially accepted the position of Operations Assistant. And then, on 26th March, I received the following correspondence:

Dear Alan
At the conclusion of the meeting to discuss restructuring the Traffic Office, I informed you that I would write to you to confirm the next stage in the procedure. Since the meeting, the possibility of significant changes to our operation has arisen, and myself and David Reeves feel that it would be prudent to wait for the outcome of these potential changes before proposing any changes to the Traffic Office that may subsequently be affected by them.
I am then, writing to advise you that what was discussed at the meeting will be suspended for the immediate future, and I will write to you again by Monday 20 April 2009 to advise you of any revised proposals, and the way forward from that point. As there were some key issues raised, I would welcome your

feedback and comments on ways in which we could improve the efficiency of the Traffic Office.
  Sincerely
  Steve Elms
  <u>*General Manager*</u>

Back to square one!
  I began working on giving my feedback, and suggestions, when an incident which occurred a little while later thoroughly incensed me, and immediately made up my mind to get out of a festering office environment.

On Good Friday (10th April), the engineering manager, Bob Lowe, took the day off to go sailing. This was a favourite hobby/pastime of Bob's, and he was entitled to have the day off as it was a bank holiday. Shaz Ali, however, didn't see it that way. He expected his staff to be at work, even on a bank holiday if he so desired them to be. In fairness, my experience of the Good Friday bank holiday was that it was treated as a normal working day, for which one would receive a day's pay as well as a bank holiday payment. But the decision was left to the individual... unless one worked under Shaz Ali!
  On the day in question, I was in the office with Dave Wilde; we were counting the drivers' cash, due to the machine being out of commission. I popped outside for some fresh air, and immediately became aware of Shaz Ali standing in the middle of the yard, near a row of parked cars. He turned, looked at me and shouted, 'I don't give a fuck for Good Friday... and I don't give a fuck for Easter Sunday, either!'
  I confronted him immediately; berating him for his outburst! What I actually said to his face was repeated in the letter I wrote to him, on Easter Sunday (see below).

Following that confrontation, I returned to the office, whereupon I said to Dave Wilde in a whispering voice: 'What I say next, mate, when Shaz comes in, please don't laugh.' He looked at me somewhat bemused, then replied, 'Yeah, okay.'

Shaz Ali came back inside and walked past our little room into his office... or the one he shared with Steve Elms, to be exact. Only a glass partition separated us. I stood up and said in a way that Ali couldn't help but hear: 'I need to go at two o'clock, mate; I've got to be in church for three pm.'

Dave sniggered quietly but held his nerve. I told him I would explain later. I did, and he agreed with me; Mr Ali was bang out of order!

I couldn't get that man's unnecessary rant out of my mind. I mulled it over for a couple of days, before deciding that enough was enough. I wrote the following at home on Easter Sunday:

Dear Shaz,

I write to inform you that following some consideration, I will not be applying for any promotional position in the traffic office that may be advertised. And to be absolutely honest with you, I have to say that your outburst at the front of the depot on Good Friday has assisted me in arriving at my decision.

You were very angry (as you said so yourself) due to an apparent problem with Engineering. But when you remarked, in a raised voice (quote): 'I don't give a fu*k for Good Friday and I don't give a fu*k for Easter Sunday either', I had to speak to you.

I was very shocked to hear this unnecessary outburst to tell you the truth.

And as I pointed out to you, most of the people who work here are Christians, be it Catholic or C of E, and Easter is the most important religious event on the Christian calendar. But you appeared not to be in the slightest bit bothered.

As the day progressed your words kept coming into my mind, so much so that I haven't been able to think of anything else since!

I thought your remarks were inappropriate, insensitive, and extremely offensive. And I can't help thinking of how you would feel, and react if I or anyone else spoke in such appalling and derogatory terms (as you did), about your chosen faith.

I do appreciate the recent chats we have had with regard to making progress here at Choice, but I do not feel that we could work together closely, again. I remain deeply hurt by your outburst which even if said in the heat of the moment, was totally unjustified. It is for me, a matter of principle, and I hope you understand.

I am therefore committed to returning to full time driving duties on the Market Drayton routes (as previously agreed) as and when it suits you. I realise this might be seen as just an excuse to return to driving because I have, in the past, made it clear that I have no desire to return to management. My reason however, is as stated above.

Saying that; I have thoroughly enjoyed my six months in the traffic office, and I do feel that I have made a positive contribution.

I wish you well in your new role.

Alan Scriven MBE

Operations Assistant

Cc Mr S Elms, General Manager; file.

When Steve Elms read his copy of the letter, first thing on the Tuesday morning he came straight out and said to me, 'You're not seriously giving him this are you, Scriv?'

'Yes,' I replied, 'why not?'

'He'll go bloody mad, you can't do this.'

'I'm doing it, Steve; make sure he gets his copy.'

I watched from the counting room as Mr Ali took possession of my letter at 0815hrs on Tuesday 14th April.

He sent for me at 1645hrs!

As I entered Shaz's office, his opening words were: 'Jesus had twelve disciples.' He then quoted all the names of the disciples before adding: 'I didn't mean what I said, you know. My wife is a Catholic.'

I couldn't forget his nasty words, though, or forgive him. So I told him I wanted to return to my place on the 341/342 Wellington to Market Drayton service, as outlined in my letter – which, I reminded him again was agreed with Dave Reeves when I took the office position. He continued with his efforts to change my mind, but it was all to no avail; I'd had enough of the bloke!

It seemed to me (and certainly to the two people involved) that Shaz Ali was desperate to get rid of Dave and Claire Wilde, and he appeared not to care who knew it! But he was getting no assistance in his dirty work from me.

Out of the blue, I was summoned to a meeting with Shaz on 3rd December 2009. I had been back on the road for approximately six months, in which time Dave Reeves had decided to 're-boot' the depot; it was now to be known as 'Midland'. Dave himself asked me to reconsider my decision to quit the traffic office, but as with Mr Ali, he got short shrift.

The reason for the meeting, as it turned out, was to advise me that my pay rate was to be reduced (due to my leaving the office) from £8.17 per hour to £7.50 (driver's rate). If he thought that might change my mind, he was wrong... again. I considered his decision to be fair; after all, I hadn't been a member of the traffic office for some considerable time.

A vacancy for an inspector was posted in January 2010. I decided to apply. Unfortunately, however, I was informed that the position was only a twenty-hour-per-week duty, and that wouldn't meet my earning requirements, so I withdrew my interest, opting to continue with my driving responsibilities. To that end, on 4th July I completed a 'Driver CPC Periodic Training' course; receiving a nice certificate from Mr Paul Moffat on behalf of D&G. A second certificate (for a similar course) followed on 12th June 2011. It was probably on this particular course (because I remember it being a very warm day) that we English drivers were shown what our Polish counterparts actually thought about these boring courses. They had brought a couple of large bottles of 'Coca-cola' into the room, and were passing them round to each other, after taking a hefty swig first. For a while, no-one thought anything of this, as we all struggled to appear interested in what Claire Wilde (who was presenting the course) was either showing us on screen, or saying. When the instructor stopped speaking, in order for us to take a break, as the Polish drivers stood up, they all but plaited their legs! Claire twigged and asked to sample the cola. But quick as a flash, the lads holding the bottles 'necked' the contents before Claire could get anywhere near them; class! But to be fair, the course was entirely in English, and there was no translator in the room. Who then, could blame them for joining us in abject disinterest? Those wastes of a day here and there continue to this day!

During the latter years of my time at Wednesfield, and under its time as a D&G depot, I was approached to take part in a television documentary (of sorts) called *The Money Programme*. The company had been approached to supply an employee to be included in the thirty-minute show, and Dave Reeves invited me to be that person. My mind went back to the day when Ian Tully and I had appeared in *Home and Away*. That had been fun, so I thought, why not? 'Great,' said Dave, 'they'll be in touch with you.' On the day of filming, I had to be at the Custard Factory in Birmingham for 9am, if memory serves. When I arrived, it was explained to us (there were lots of other people there representing a variety of trades and professions) that a panel of judges would be formed from our number, and the remainder would each have some time to attempt to convince the panel that they or their chosen profession should receive the largest slice of a set amount of money in remuneration for their skills. I was chosen to be a panel member. The television newsreader Sophie Raworth presented (she's even more beautiful in the flesh), and she was brilliant and very professional. To cut a long story short, all the professions or trades people stated their case to us and after quite some time deliberating, we chose the plumber. Well, the plumber is on call 24/7 and in all weathers. I think we gave the doctor second place, followed by the nurse and the bricklayer. The architect went berserk! He rounded on me because I had delivered the result. 'I should have the most money, not these,' he protested, 'you have no idea what you're talking about.'

I replied with a slap of my own hand saying, 'Well hush my mouth.' Sophie Raworth burst into laughter, called for the camera to stop rolling – I had forgotten that it was – and said to me, 'That was brilliant, let's do that again, Alan.' The posh architect was not impressed, and I thought he might want to finish the row outside; I would have been up for that, but after filming he just slunk away and out of the premises. And when it was all 'in the can' as we television stars (?) say, I shared a taxi back to the train station with Sophie.

Chapter Eleven

The Market Drayton Run

As I mentioned earlier, I worked on the 341/342 Wellington to Market Drayton routes for almost six years during my time at Wednesfield, and I really enjoyed it. When Choice Travel acquired the service from Arriva, I was already familiar with it from my long spell at wonderful Wellington. This, however, didn't stop me from joining a group of drivers who were taken out on a Sunday morning for five hours' route learning... I sat on the rear seat of the Optare Solo bus, paying not the slightest bit of attention to the route instruction. I remember Shirley Brunyee saying to her husband Tony, 'He already knows the route.' Correct, Shirley, but five hours' pay wasn't to be sniffed at!

I was therefore invited to be one of the two drivers asked to operate the routes on the first day of service in 2005. And from that day, I became the one driver who would work daily on the 'Drayton run' during the six years that it operated out of Wednesfield depot (with the exception of my short term as Operations Assistant/Assistant Manager). Then after a while, Rob Harris became the other regular driver... until he suddenly left the company, giving Surinder Grewal the opportunity to take his place on a regular basis. Rob and I didn't see eye to eye when I initially joined Choice Travel, but after a 'clear the air' chat, we became good friends, and we still are today. Rob is a cousin of Simon Harris, whom I also worked with at Wednesfield, and currently work with at Select Bus Services.

I worked well with both Rob and Surinder, and we got to know our regular passengers, some of whom became friends. In fact, when the service was returned to Arriva in 2011, some of the more regular passengers and I made a pact to meet up in Wellington at certain times throughout the following years. We called our little group 'the 341ers' and our meetings took place at the William Withering public house; until the Coronavirus (or Covid-19) pandemic so rudely interrupted normal life. It stopped everyone in their tracks! But now that all Covid restrictions have been lifted, we have resumed our meetings in Wellington.

The 'Drayton run' brought me into contact with some very interesting and funny people; one of the latter being Ray from Stoke-on-Tern. He used to dress like Compo (from that hilarious BBC comedy series *Last of the Summer Wine*), and he didn't care a jot what anyone thought. Ray would board the bus and immediately start singing out loud. His two favourite songs, which I often accompanied him in, were *The Black Hills of Dakota*, and *Red River Valley*. A neighbour of his, Cheryl, was a friend of Trudy Hutchinson (a passenger on the 341 service who I now count as a friend), and what a character she was! Sadly, both Cheryl and Ray are lost to us now. Trudy, from Stoke-on-Tern, still works at the Princess Royal Hospital in Wellington, and is a constant at our renewed meetings in Wellington.

Nick Winkler, a young man from Childs Ercall (and an Asperger's sufferer) stuck to me like the proverbial sh*t to a blanket; following me everywhere whenever I was on a break in Wellington. His parents were of German nationality, and they decided to return to their homeland some years ago now, taking Nick with them. But I still hear from Nick on my birthday, and at Christmas; Angie Roberts, from Waters Upton, another member of our group, is more frequently in touch with Nick.

An elderly gent called Peter Cook, also from Childs Ercall, was a daily passenger in and out of Wellington. Sadly, and for no apparent reason, he boarded the last bus (my 1650hrs) one day from Wellington, and instead of alighting at his usual stop, he continued his journey a little way further, asking to be set down between Childs Ercall and Ollerton. When he eventually left the bus, Pete's last words to me were: 'Tell Sarah to behave.' Sarah was a young neighbour of Pete's, who used regularly to travel into Wellington with him. A few days after Pete made what turned out to be his final journey, his body was pulled out of the nearby Peplow pool. Such a sad loss: Cookie was a good old stick, with no obvious concerns about life. But his tragic end just goes to show that no-one really knows what goes on in the minds of others. I attended his funeral at Peplow, and was pleasantly surprised to hear the vicar say that Pete had featured in a book; I love to hear stuff about the achievements of people. He hailed from the Wirrall, did Peter. Good old stick.

The ladies on that brilliant run included Angie Roberts (mentioned above), Gwen, Karen and Ruth from Waters Upton; Margaret Brown and her daughter Becky from Wellington, who still stable horses at Waters Upton, ably assisted in the stables by Margaret's husband Barry, a now happily retired postal worker.

From Childs Ercall, a nice lady called Christine was a regular on the morning service to her job in Market Drayton; travelling with (amongst others) Mrs Winters, a well-known elderly character who invited me to call her Cassandra.

Trudy Hutchinson (as mentioned above) and her daughter Beth were very regular passengers, along with Trudy's daughter-in-law Emma. When I began working on that lovely service, Beth was a small child attending the local primary school at Stoke-on-Tern. I took her to school all through those years, and now she is a mother herself. One day, Trudy and Beth were waiting at the Dutton Close bus stop for the 341; and as usual, I was running a little late due to the people of the various villages and hamlets stopping me for a chat, or even to ask me to deliver items (usually fresh foodstuff and the like) to someone in the next village. Trudy was apparently growing evermore irritable at my lateness. Beth later told me that her mother had remarked (light-heartedly) on my lateness: 'I bet it's fucking Alan again.'

Mrs Lister from Hodnet, who travelled on our 342 service, always had an apple for me; and she also gave me cuttings of plants from her ample garden at various times of the year.

There was also Mick, his wife, and their daughter Jane, from Ollerton. And I must mention the farmer from that small hamlet; Phil Harris. He was getting on a bit, but as sharp as a sailor's knife! We met one morning in a very narrow lane. I politely asked him to reverse... and he very politely refused!

'Oh no, cock, I never reverse for buses; nothing personal, mind, I just don't do it,' he said from the comfort of his driving seat. I asked him again to back his small van into a cut-out just a few yards behind. He was most gracious in his second refusal, despite me saying that I could not reverse the bus. 'What we gonna do then, kid?' he asked with a wry smile.

I'd had enough. 'Okay' I said, 'I'll ring the police because you're causing an obstruction. And when they arrive, we'll see which one of us they make reverse.'

That did the trick, as it invariably does whenever bus drivers meet oncoming vehicles in very narrow lanes. He reversed, then got out of his little green van, and shook my hand as I slowly passed. And from that day on, he always reversed whenever we met, which was frequently. Phil and I became friends: he even kindly allowed my friend John Preece and I to do some metal-detecting on his land.

Actually, this reminds me of the time I asked Nick Winkler (mentioned previously) for permission to do some detecting in the field, or garden around his family's house; the former vicarage in Childs Ercall. I am reliably informed that fairs were held on fields next to a vicarage or church in Victorian times; could be a goldmine, I thought. Nick assured me that he would speak to his parents. These were his actual words after doing so: 'My dad said yes you can, but he wants to follow you round as you do it.' I asked Nick why his father wanted to do this. He replied, 'Because he doesn't trust you.' Well, people with Autism tell it like it is! I never did take his father up, on his 'kind' offer. Not because I didn't want Mr Winkler to witness any findings; I just didn't fancy him peering over my shoulder every time I received a signal.

Dave Evans, from Eaton-on-Tern, and his cousin, along with their mothers, were regulars on the 341. They lived next door to each other in that pretty little village.

I apologise to anyone – during this period of my career – that I may have forgotten to mention.

Seemingly from nowhere, the end of the Market Drayton run, for us at Midland, had galloped into our operations. It was a sad day for Surinder, me, and our wonderful passengers. On the final day of service at 07:02 hrs, I drove fleet no 1102, an Optare Solo in the red livery of Midland, into Wellington Bus Station. Barry Brown (mentioned previously) stood in the bus shelter. He told me he wasn't catching the bus, just waiting for someone... Following a brief chat about the family's horses; and the fact that everyone was gutted (not least of all myself) about the demise of the service, I departed. Throughout that day, regular passengers and former colleagues were remarking (with mixed opinions) about this day being significant.

At 1510hrs, I drove out of Wellington for the final time as a driver on the 341/342 service. I had a few passengers, all of whom expressed their sadness that our company had lost the service to Arriva. It meant, they said, a return to 'a regimental style of service', meaning their drivers would 'stick to the book' regarding boarding and alighting. You may remember me mentioning earlier how drivers hate the 'hail and ride' system operated on some routes. The dislike of this, however, is by and large reserved for town runs. Country routes such as the Market Drayton run had to offer 'hail and ride' where necessary.

The passengers said that Surinder and I would be sorely missed; that was a nice and an appreciative summary of how well we were thought of. The service has disappeared completely now, apparently, after Arriva withdrew the one bus per day, which took an age to get its passengers into town.

As I drove into Waters Upton village, a short way past Angela and Huw Roberts' house, I noticed a couple of familiar faces standing in the lane outside the village hall. They tried to guide me onto the car park, but I stopped and told them that the service had to continue to Childs Ercall. Imagine my shock when I was politely informed that my bosses had given the green light for me to terminate the service at the hall, so that a number of passengers, from various parts of the route, could thank me for my service, with an impromptu farewell party! I had never experienced anything like it; it was both touching, and brilliant; and I remain, to this day, very grateful for their extraordinary kindness. Barry Brown explained that the real reason he was stood in the bus shelter at the start of my duty was simply to make sure that I was actually at work on the final day of service. He then gave the information to the ladies, so that the room could be arranged. How nice was that.

I made a bit of a speech; one or two got a little teary, but we all enjoyed that short time together.

I left them with a promise that we would all keep in touch... and up until the Coronavirus pandemic struck, we did. And now Rob Harris is a member of our group, I'm sure our days together will be brilliant!

My years on that great service included a couple of serious accidents, sadly, which I will include in the final chapter. Generally speaking, however, life was a bowl of cherries. I was away from the stresses of management again, and feeling much better for it. Saying that, maybe if Dave Reeves hadn't invited Shaz Ali to join as a director at Wednesfield, I may well have continued in an office-based role. Ironically, by this stage in my Wednesfield tenure, Shaz was no longer with the company, or at least not at Wednesfield.

Chapter Twelve

Dark Days Ahead!

Mr Ali made it painfully obvious to everyone – even the directors and senior management at Midland, which our depot had now become following a re-brand that included a merger with A2Z Transport Services (hence the Ali factor) – that he didn't trust his office team. He was taking some time off at the beginning of 2011, and rather than leave the office staff to 'man the fort', he arranged with Dave Reeves for Kevin Crawford (manager at the Longton depot) to come down to Wednesfield and keep his beady eyes on us all! Shaz may even have suggested that the office staff were incapable of keeping the ship afloat whilst he was away. Big mistake!

Kevin arrived quietly (just after Shaz began his holiday) under the title of Operations Manager, and he allowed the place to tick over, as it had, with no problems whatsoever. He kept out of the day-to-day running, but obviously and quite naturally fulfilled his required role of observation. The result was that Shaz's services were dispensed with, leaving Kevin to become a very welcome full-time member of the team.

Kevin, a really likeable Trevor Brooking lookalike (in my eyes at least), wrote to all members of Wednesfield staff on 'Trafalgar Day', 21st October (2011). I love Admiral Lord Horatio Nelson; he is in my eyes the greatest Englishman who ever lived. Not just for the battle of Trafalgar, which sadly claimed his life just at the moment of victory, but all the previous maritime battles he won for his country. Another maritime idol of mine is Captain William Bligh (who served with Nelson before the infamous mutiny). If his great seamanship qualities weren't appreciated before the mutiny, they certainly were afterwards. And he actually wasn't the ogre that history has painted him as!

The gist of Kevin's correspondence was to inform us that, generally speaking, he was happy with how the depot had operated during the nine months he had been with us. Not difficult, really, when you have someone at the helm you can trust, and who trusts you!

I had the privilege, along with Dave Wilde, and Claire's father (and one or two others, including Kev's son) of accompanying Kevin on a trip to Wembley to watch an England versus Scotland game. He's a great guy, and still doing a brilliant job for D&G Bus and Coach back at Longton.

On 14th November 2011, I received notice from Tim Jeffcoat (mentioned earlier) that a 'Mystery Customer' (or some nosy twat paid by the company to spy on the drivers) had travelled on my bus (service 57 on Friday 21st October, Trafalgar Day), and reported back to the office commenting on my smart appearance and polite manner. I have never agreed with using these people! I had my fair share of reports whilst an Arriva manager, from one Carol Henderson, mainly. She would actually whisper to me on the phone: 'Can you come and meet me in the cafe at Cannock Bus Station because I have another report for you.' Invariably, it was something and nothing, which I dealt with, on most occasions, without even involving the driver concerned.

Being now a part of D&G brought me into contact with one Chris Almond. He would visit our Wednesfield depot as part of his scheduling responsibilities and all the other (traffic related) work he did. Chris is a nice guy who I again linked up with when I joined Select Bus Services later in my career, when the Julian Peddle factor brought both companies a little closer.

The year ended with Heidi Holland (D&G Transport Manager) writing to me on 5th December, informing me that I was to attend another boring CPC session on Sunday 15th January 2012. What an absolute waste of a rest day! Starting at 0900hrs, someone would stand in front of us spouting crap about stuff we already knew; or crap that didn't concern us, until at least 1600hrs... if we were lucky! This session was squashed between one on 8th January, and a third, which took place on Sunday 5th August. In the meantime, Dave Wilde's position and title had been changed to 'Administration Manager', whatever that meant!

It was during my time at Wednesfield that I came into contact again with an old school friend, who was working as a driver for NX based at Park Lane depot. Chris Bennett and I had been good mates during our childhood. He lived in Goodyear Avenue, just a stone's throw from our house in Fifth Avenue. Chris wasn't as keen on football as I was, so we didn't see much of each other during the evenings, but he was a good mate nonetheless, whom I still see out and about occasionally, with his lady wife.

During the early summer of 2012, rumours were rife that Dave Reeves was in negotiations with a view to selling Wednesfield Depot to my former employers (and nemesis) Arriva! On every occasion, however, when I or anyone else attempted to 'squeeze the grapevine', we were given the same cold-shoulder response: 'Don't know what you're talking about.' And then suddenly we were all invited to attend a meeting at the Polish Club, Stafford Road, Oxley, in north Wolverhampton. The evening's shock events revealed that Reeves had in fact sold us (down the river)... to Arriva. Shit!

So after nine very happy (on the whole) years at Wednesfield, I was back in the doldrums. We became a part of Arriva on Monday 17th September 2012, with Mark Wynne being appointed General Manager by Alf Lloyd (Customer Operations Director).

At that meeting at the Polish Club, we were asked if we had any questions. Before anyone could respond, Dave Reeves jumped in and asked, on my behalf, if drivers would be allowed to continue wearing shorts. A very swift 'NO' was the response, with the following: 'I'm sure Mr Scriven remembers our policy on this issue.' As I said above; my decision whilst Traffic Manager at Wellington returned to haunt me. I had worn shorts every day during my time as a driver at Wednesfield; alas, however, not anymore – at least not for the next four years!

Sadly, Dave Reeves' very kind parting gift of a handsome bonus did nothing to ease my feelings of dread at becoming an employee of Arriva again. The following is my letter of thanks to Mr Reeves:

Dear Dave

I wanted to say on record how very grateful I am for the extra money you kindly gave me with my final wages from D&G. You said it was for my efforts and hard work.

Well thank you very much for that Dave, and for sticking with us through the lean times.

For myself, it was a pleasure to work for you; and I really enjoyed our conversations, and the faith you showed in my (to quote you) "professionalism and ability."

I'm very sorry that I let you down in the office, but truth to tell, I couldn't have worked in there with you know who one more day!

Thanks again Dave, and I wish you every success with your ongoing business ventures.

Yours sincerely
Alan ('Scriv').

Mark Wynne was replaced as General Manager by a certain Mr Raj Chander in January 2013. Raj wrote to each of us on Monday 4th March, advising that the Office of Fair Trading had given Arriva Midlands clearance to fully complete the purchase of 'Liyall Ltd, trading as Midland'. Terrible news!

The *Arriva NOW!* magazine was still in production, and its March 2013 edition included a double-page feature of the takeover news, and a profile of Raj Chander.

He had joined the company from National Express, where he had served (most recently) as an operations manager. In the article, he is quoted as saying, 'There is a very friendly atmosphere at the depot, and everyone is geared up and excited about working for Arriva Midlands.' Not everyone was, Raj!

At the time of the invasion – sorry, *takeover* – Wednesfield was operating a total of thirty-five routes; I was familiar with just seven of them because of my six years on the Market Drayton routes. And following that service's return to Arriva Wellington, I stuck mainly to services 10, 63, 64 and 65. My time as the regular driver of the 18 service, combined with a college run to Stafford from Cheslyn Hay (via Cannock and Hednesford) was waiting for me in the near future.

At the time of Arriva's move into Wednesfield, the depot had a fleet of fifty-five buses, with a total staff of 108, of which eighty-one were drivers. During the meeting at the Polish club (as mentioned above), Keith Myatt, Arriva Midlands publicity officer, and a man I knew very well from my previous time with the company, sidled up to me, and asked me what I thought of the takeover. I replied: 'Well, Keith, I suppose I have to look for the positives.' He beamed, and said, excitedly, 'Yes that's right Scriv.' Our cosy chat ended quickly, however, when I added: 'God knows how long I'll be looking, though!' He wandered off again.

The magazine also included a small picture of my old mate from Wellington, John 'Trubby' Trubshaw. He was (at that time) the depot's engineering manager, and had been mentioned for his work in getting the new Telford depot, at Stafford Park, set up. Trubby was also a valued volunteer under my leadership of the Longmynd Adventure Camp, back in the 1990s.

As I was still a member of the Wednesfield Works Committee, I attended a meeting on 19th March 2013 (the twenty-sixth anniversary of my mother's death), to discuss a new 'schedules and wages package' following the merging of Hill Top depot's services with ours. In effect, all of its work and drivers came to join Wednesfield. Financially, Hill Top was underperforming, and had won none of the recently advertised tenders. The proposed package was as follows:

	Current	Proposed
Basic hourly rate	£7:45	£7:55
Sunday rate	£8:15	£8:15
Mon – Sat (after 1900hrs)	£7:95	£7:55
Sunday (after 1900hrs)	£8:45	£8:15
Guaranteed day Mon/Sat	n/a	7.0hrs
Guaranteed day (Sun)	n/a	5.0hrs
Guaranteed week	38hrs	38hrs
Signing on time	5mins	10mins
Except when not taking bus out	5mins	5mins
Signing off time	0mins	2mins
Max single unpaid break (During Shift)	40mins	75mins

In between the meeting to discuss and then implement the changes on 28th April (following approval from the Works Committee), I received notification on 10th April 2014 from Claire Wilde, who now occupied the position of Duty Manager (along with Dave Wilde, Adam French, and Gurdeep Samplay) that I was expected to partake in some (new) route learning. I politely refused, saying I was happy with what I was currently doing. That didn't go down too well, but hey ho!

Jack Grove – whom I had known previously during my time at wonderful Wellington – was now Operations Assistant (taking over my previous position) and on 9th December he wrote to me, 'inviting' me to attend an 'informal chat' regarding another covert check on me, on 28ᵗʰ November 2013. I was working on service 19 Wolverhampton to Walsall. And as with the most previous 'spy checks' on me, it was reported that I had been most professional in every aspect of my responsibilities. But a short while later, I was again invited up to Jack's office; this time, to discuss apparent damage to a bus I was driving around the Brinsford estate on service 67, which today is operated by my current employers Select Bus Services. Whilst passing two council tipper trucks on a left-hand bend, I had caused one of the battery cover clips to become (quote) 'misshaped' by the grass bank to my offside. Misshaped? Before beginning the very tight manoeuvre, I went looking for the drivers, but they were nowhere to be seen. I explained all this to Jack, but grew increasingly angry at his condescending attitude, to the point that I stood up and said, 'Jack, with all due respect to you and your position, I have to say that at your young age, and the short time you have been in this game; what you actually know about the industry, I could carve on the back of an aspirin. You don't possess a licence of the kind required to be qualified to talk to me about issues on the road.'

Perhaps to his credit, he responded thus: 'Okay Scriv, fuck off!'

A while later, Claire Wilde asked me to take on the 837 Stafford college run. It would be operated before and after the 18 service (as mentioned above), which began on the Lyndurst estate in Wednesfield at 09:30hrs. The 18 route ran to Wolverhampton via Wednesfield village, and the service would terminate back at Lyndurst at 14:30hrs. A break at the depot followed before I drove to the college for the return journey to Cheslyn Hay via Cannock Chase, Hednesford, Cannock bus station and Great Wyrley.

Claire and I went out to have a look at the 837 run, and after working out the Cheslyn Hay one-way system, I agreed to do it. So for five days a week, I operated the 837 and 18 services, and the standalone 18 on a Saturday. I really enjoyed every aspect of that duty: college kids to start and end my day, with the 'silver surfers' wedged in between!

Yet one more certificate was presented to me at the end of 2014; a 'Safe Driving Diploma' from the council, in respect of yet another whole year free from blameworthy accidents.

One morning in 2015, however, I arrived for work to find Claire Wilde holding a copy of a photograph showing a severely damaged tyre. After handing it to me, she asked, 'Do you know anything about this, Scriv?' I replied (truthfully) in the negative. She then gave me an incident report form and asked me to put in writing what I had just told her. I did so and returned the completed form to her, thinking no more about it. Five weeks later, however, I received notification of a formal conduct hearing (regarding the damaged tyre) to be chaired by Raj Chander. By this time in his tenure at Wednesfield, we had developed a 'love-hate' kind of working relationship: I loved hating him! He was openly rude, ignorant, and obnoxious to most of the people who were employed at that once happy little depot. He had the proverbial chip on his shoulder the size of Gibraltar!

Raj opened the hearing by asking me if I wanted representation; I declined. He asked why not; I told him I didn't need it. He then began to formally appraise me of the reason for this cosy little chat. Showing me the same picture that Claire had put under my nose a few weeks back, he asked me the same question that she had. I gave a similar reply. He began trying to press me into admitting to causing the damage. My response, in no uncertain terms, was that a) I was not responsible, b) any driver worth his/her salt would realise that the severity of damage was likely to get the depot closed, let alone what penalty the guilty driver would face, and c) why was he pointing the finger at me? His reply to this was: 'Well, the other two drivers that had the bus on the same day have said it wasn't them!' Oh, I see; it had to be me then. Err, no way!'

He continued, stating that the person responsible should be awarded a written warning at least. I replied in agreement, adding, 'Well, when you find that person, Raj, go for it.' I then said, 'I suppose you'll want to adjourn for a while to consider your decision. But before you do, let me just say this. I could look you in the eye right now and tell you to your face that I was responsible for that damaged tyre... and there's nothing you could do about it, because you're out of procedure. The damage was caused at least five weeks ago.' I told him that I had sat on his side of the desk during my illustrious career (he didn't like that) and I knew employment law very well. He didn't appreciate that either, or everything else I said appertaining to my previous experience. He wasn't going to get away with railroading me!

'Well you have been on holiday,' he replied. Unbelievable! I'd had one week's holiday!

I stood up and said, 'Call me back in when you're ready.'

About ten minutes later, he did just that, and before saying I was right, that he couldn't do anything (even if I was guilty) because of the time delay, he sarcastically quoted me word for word almost, on what I had said regarding my previous managerial positions, before leaving his office at the point of adjournment.

Case dismissed. My parting shot was to remind him that I had been the second driver, and I had asked the third driver to have a walk round the bus before taking it over. I drove that bus for exactly one hour out of the nine or so that it was in service! He was just looking to make me his scapegoat. No chance!

Mr Chander thought for whatever reason that he could pin the blame on me, but he got just a little bit more than he bargained for. I've often wondered why he was so obviously against me and I reckon it must have been a little insecurity on his part. In total contrast, by the way, he thought the sun shone out of Claire Wilde's backside; and the feeling was mutual!

From that day forward, I knew that I was probably a marked

man again! I hadn't joined the union, so if I did get formally invited upstairs again, I would have to defend myself, again. No worries; I had, from past experience, a good knowledge of employment law, so looking after myself wouldn't present too many problems, especially if I continued to do my very best during every working day, as I always had. And that's how my final full year at Wednesfield ended.

The new year got off to a promising start; I was enjoying my work and despite the later rumours that the garage was closing, or another imminent take-over was on the cards, we all got on with our jobs. During the early summer, however, I was involved in a road traffic accident (RTA) which ultimately brought about the end of my Arriva career, for a second and final time.
Every cloud...

This is my letter to Raj Chander, submitting my resignation, which I copied to the now late Mr R. Cheveaux (Area MD) dated 5th August 2016, by which time I had been offered employment at Select Bus Services Ltd of Penkridge, Stafford:

Dear Sir
   It is with <u>*some*</u> *regret that I ask you to accept this correspondence as one week's notice of my intention to terminate my employment with Arriva Midlands (Wednesfield), in accordance with my contractual obligations.*
   My final day of work will be Friday 12 August 2016.
   I have to say that (in my opinion) the very severe and unnecessarily harsh penalty, awarded by your assistant Mr P Wilkes (whom I have nothing against personally) for my recent accident, has without doubt, contributed heavily to my decision to leave; although I realise that you won't be shedding any tears... I'm not that naive.
   I have worked at this depot for just over thirteen years,

latterly in my second spell with Arriva, and up until my appointment with Mr Wilkes recently, held a clean conduct record throughout, and a (blameworthy) accident free record.

You may wonder why I did not appeal against his decision to award a FWW. Well I'm sorry to say Mr Chander, but I considered then, as I do now, that I would not have succeeded in getting the award reduced, especially considering that you yourself was going to hear the appeal (more than a probability). I say this because I have never felt that you have been a fair and professional manager, and to be honest, that is the opinion of the majority of people working here at Wednesfield; and I do mean drivers, office staff and engineers.

But I suppose you must already be aware of that yourself, if you're honest.

My first real experience of your 'unique style' of management was the occasion when you required me to attend a formal conduct hearing over a torn tyre; do you remember? You read out my negative written response to the question as to whether I knew anything about the damage. Then you asked if I still stood by my response... or did I "wish to change it". I told you that I had no wish to change it, because my initial response was the truth!

I had a notion of how you thought you were going to resolve this when you said (unbelievably) that the other two drivers "said they didn't do it". Oh right; so it had to be me then.......

I was the second driver of three to take responsibility of that bus on that day. I had it for precisely one hour, and the third driver walked around it in my presence. Nothing untoward was found, as I told you at the hearing.

I asked you if you had looked at my personal file, because if you had done so you would have seen that I am very experienced in this industry having occupied all positions on the traffic side of the business, with the exception of allocation of duties.

I said that I was well aware of what the consequences to both the depot and the driver would have been, had VOSA, or indeed the police noticed the extent of the damage to the tyre whilst the vehicle was in service. But having invited me to comment, all you did was rudely speak over me and interrupt; a definite sign of weakness, insecurity and a lack of professionalism. In fact, in my honest opinion, your personnel skills are zero, and to be absolutely frank, I think you are a bully!

Having listened again to your rant about awarding a WW "in the very least" to the person responsible (me in your eyes) I had heard enough. So I pointed out that the hearing was actually nul and void due to you being out of procedure, owing to the passage of time between the damage being caused, and the formal hearing. You then tried to argue your case by saying that I had been on holiday. But, as I reminded you: I had been on holiday for one week not five! I added that I had not aspired to the positions I have held in this industry through being an idiot.

You adjourned.

On reconvening, you sarcastically repeated my words regarding the above, and quoted me on what I said about my considerable level of experience in the industry, before ungraciously sending me on my way grudgingly, with my good conduct record still intact... obviously though with more than a hint of revenge in your thoughts!

Why you so obviously and blatantly attempted to pin the blame on me, I don't know. But from that moment on, I knew it was just a matter of time before you found something else to try and nail me for.

I don't usually boast about my qualities... but what insight!

I wish you every success in your ongoing career.

I trust that all monies owed to me on my leaving date will be paid, subject to my returning all items of company property in accordance with Arriva company policy.

Yours faithfully

Alan Scriven MBE

Whether to the man's credit or not; I was informed by Claire Wilde that he fully accepted, and even agreed with, everything I had said in this correspondence.
A tad cocky or condescending, perhaps!

Chapter Thirteen

Pastures Greener

After discovering from my family history research that my maternal ancestors were agricultural workers, born and bred in Claverley, Shropshire, back in the 1800s, I had wanted to work on a farm myself, and in August 2016 I got my wish... in a manner of speaking!

One morning (a short time after that 'meeting' with Phil Lewis), just as I pulled up at the bus stop in Lichfield Street, Wolverhampton, on the 18 service, I met Simon Harris. Simon and I, as mentioned previously, had been friends since our time together at Wednesfield. He was now working for Select Bus Services in Penkridge, near the county town of Staffordshire, and had pulled in behind me on the 67 service (Wolves to Cannock). His first words to me were, 'Hey Scriv, fancy a job at our place?' He went on to tell me that his boss, a young man by the name of Ben Brown, had mentioned that he had a vacancy for a driver. 'He knows all about you, Scriv, and he's asked me to ask you, if I saw you about.'

I was a little taken aback. I didn't realise that Ben Brown 'knew me'. I had heard about him via the industry bongo drums, but I didn't actually know the man. However, a piece of paper which he handed to me not long ago proved that our paths had indeed crossed.

My situation at Arriva was growing ever more precarious after the little chit-chat with Chander's sidekick, and the totally unfair Final Written Warning that had resulted from it. I asked Simon if he was sure about what he was saying to me. He confirmed, and then gave me Ben's number. 'Give him a bell,

Scriv, he's waiting for your call.'

Simon Harris wasn't the only ex-Wednesfield driver who was now doing the business for Ben at Select. There was also the 'gentle giant' (to quote Chris Kent) that is Tony Brunyee. Tony, along with his wife Shirley, was a driver-clerk at Choice when I joined. If you don't know Tony, you're missing out. He is one of the nicest guys you will ever meet; always calm, with a very pleasant disposition, and extremely helpful when you need him. Tony joined Select in 2014. Currently, Shirley works two days a week, also at Select.

I thanked Simon for the information, and said I would give it some thought. Well, it was potentially a very risky chance to take, even with the dire prospects at Wednesfield; and my own now precarious position. Select was a very small bus company, as far as I was aware, which a very young Ben Brown had started out in business on 11th April 2011, at the tender age of just twenty-one years. He commenced his business with just three buses and one full-time driver; a former colleague of Ben's from Green Bus Service (of Cheslyn Hay), which had been under the ownership of the outlandish, one and only Mr Graham Martin. A special kind of character, was Graham! And it didn't take me long to discover that Ben is his absolute 'doppelganger' as far as style of management goes.

The lone driver was Brian Johnson, who worked for Ben until his retirement at the young age of just seventy-five years!

Ben's working life actually began as an apprentice engineer at Arriva (Cannock), a few years after my time there as manager. Stan Kendall, who was part of the engineering team during my tenure as PSM, gave him his opportunity, but like so many others, Ben soon found out that it would have been a much better working environment in the Russian gulags! So he made a wise choice... he quit!

Nick Howes, another former Green Bus driver, started working at Select in March 2013, followed by two of Tony's (and my) friends from Wednesfield; Angie Barratt, and of course Simon Harris. Ben also employed the services of Chris Kent, who had arrived from Green Bus, via Sovereign Coaches, and Martin Elson, who joined as a driver on 17th February 2014.

I rang Ben that same afternoon; we had quite a long chat, resulting in him kindly offering me a driving position (which was all I was looking for) there and then. I asked him if I could wear shorts (I love my shorts; a 'throwback' from my many years with the Longmynd Adventure Camp). Ben answered positively, so I was buzzing! I wrote my resignation letter (as previously included) on Friday 5th August 2016, and left the employment of Arriva, for the second and final time, on Friday 12th August; my eldest son Marc's fortieth birthday.

Now having left Arriva, the doubts began to set in. I started to question whether I had done the right thing, or had I been a little hasty? The fact of the matter was, however, Arriva Wednesfield was on its last legs, and I needed to get out whilst the going was good. I actually hated what Wednesfield Depot had become under Chander's rule, and I wasn't alone in that opinion. But it has to be said that my good friend Claire Wilde didn't share my view! She and Chander rubbed along just fine, and as long as he is managing a depot somewhere, Claire is always sure of employment... and that's not a bad thing, I concede. As I write, however, she is happy to be Ben's depot manager. And as far as I know, everyone at Select Bus Services is happy that she is.

Following Ben's instructions, I found my way, on 16th August 2016, to the tiny depot, situated in a small field on Lower Drayton Farm, which lies between Penkridge and Dunston. The farm is owned and run by a very amiable (in farmer terms) Ray Bower, assisted by his son Richard and a team of people dedicated, these days, to Ray's new and growing business of a fun centre, and play opportunities for children. I have visited the Play Barn, and can definitely recommend it as a very entertaining venue for families.

As I swung my car into the field, I was met by a man whom I later discovered to be (Engineering Manager) Mike Brown, Ben's father. He directed me to the next field, where I was advised to park. To be honest, I was shocked at my surroundings. How could this place be a bus depot? Mike showed me where to go to meet Ben, who was standing in the small yard, which housed just a few buses and a couple of portacabins. Ben quickly showed me around, and then said I would be going out with Martin Elson to have a re-cap on the 67 service (which I had worked on at Wednesfield) and then more route-learning would follow, as and when the opportunity presented itself.

I had noticed Martin operating the no. 67 service during my time on route 18, when I worked at Wednesfield. From 2016, however, he became a duty manager of sorts, although I gather the change to his responsibilities wasn't actually announced formally. Moreover, Ben told me that Martin was the only person to show any interest when an office position became available, shortly before my employment began. These days, everyone accepts Martin as duty manager, because his main responsibility is to ensure on a daily basis that all duties are covered; meaning a driver for each one. I have always said that this is the most difficult job at a bus depot, and one I am grateful for never having had to do. And whatever anyone may think of Martin Elson (and we have had a couple of disagreements over the years), he always does his very best to please, and accommodate everyone, as Martin Bufton had done all those years ago, at wonderful Wellington. So obviously if Martin is able to meet a driver's needs regarding his/her working duties, he is an invaluable friend... BUT... if he has to say no, and it happens occasionally due to the very nature of the industry, he becomes public enemy no.1 for a while! So as I say, I am very grateful that during all my years in this crazy industry, I have never had the unwanted responsibility of covering the daily duties. And it doesn't matter if the depot operates a 'rolling rota' system or not, because there will always be the occasional headache for people like Martin Elson.

Over the next few days, I was introduced to Nick Howes (self-appointed 'no.1 driver'). Nick made me feel very welcome, and we became friends immediately. He, Tony Brunyee and Chris Kent operated the 'lanes duties' on a daily basis. Ben's services 877 and 878 wound their merry way through some very narrow lanes, which offer amazing countryside scenery between their start and finishing points.

Each of them gave me their personal opinion of Ben, and what it was like to work for him. And over the ensuing years, I have found that they were, in the main, correct. I have found Select Bus Services a great place to work, and for (most of the time) Ben a lenient and very generous boss who always supports his drivers whenever he considers them to be in the right, should a complaint be made against them. So by and large a favourable gaffer, although during the time that I have worked at Select, we have had a couple of ding-dong rows; both of us giving our all, standing toe to toe! If I was asked to describe Graham Martin – sorry, Ben Brown (he will take that as a compliment I hope) – I would say that he blows up... and then he blows over! A nightmare on the phone, though, if one happens to have a problem with a bus...

It took me a bit of a while to settle down at Select, if I am honest. The easy-going pace of the place was hard to come to terms with, after the almost-military style of Raj Chander, and Arriva. Some people reading that last sentence might hold the opinion that it was just the same when I was a boss at Arriva; I accept that, but I don't think I was ever as rude and obnoxious as Raj could be... on a regular basis!

In my first week at Select, I worked a total of fifty-seven hours, which gave me a net wage of £413.22. This working pattern was set to continue, and that suited me, as I had always been used to working a six-day week as a driver. These days, however, being a bit longer in the tooth, I prefer to work just four days whenever the opportunity allows, and Martin Elson to his credit always accommodates my wishes as and when he can.

Jamie Aston – or to use Ben's nickname for him, 'Duck Egg' – became a full-time driver (at least for a while) at about the same time as me, although he was part of the depot team prior to my arrival. Jamie was fresh from National Express, and the youngster of the depot, with me being the eldest, but we have got along together really well. Being the 'baby' of the depot, Jamie was (still is) the butt of some outrageous pranks, which were usually planned and executed by Ben, and Chris Kent. One day, Ben and Chris completely wrapped Jamie's car in cellophane; on another occasion, raw fish was put into the car's heating system. It was quite a while before Jamie sussed out what had been done... or was he told... eventually!? He's a great lad, Jamie; I like him a lot. And as he and Ben are best friends and about the same tender age, you'll often see one chasing the other around the yard; Ben Brown usually has the BB gun (no pun intended), with Jamie the hapless target!

One Sunday, we all went out on a bus to have a look at the 71 route, which we were about to take over from Arriva Cannock. Chris threw Jamie's trainers through one of the windows somewhere along Wood End Road in Wednesfield. Ben refused to stop the bus (saying later that he didn't hear the request) so that Jamie could retrieve them. Arriving at Cannock Bus Station, I walked the bare-footed youngster to Cannock Shopping Centre, where I bought him a new pair of trainers; all good fun.

After a short while working at Select, Ben asked me if I fancied working in the lanes. He meant did I want to try out the duties which operated, as mentioned above, out in the South Staffs countryside. I jumped at it, because it took me back to my time on the Market Drayton routes from the Wednesfield depot; six years during which I really enjoyed being a part of this crazy industry. Tony Brunyee quite rightly considered that the lanes wouldn't faze me.

A few of my former colleagues initially looked twice whenever they saw me driving a Select bus. And they took the piss a time or two, but the truth is, they would have given their eye teeth to be able to work in such a comfortable environment, and atmosphere (most of the time). In point of fact, many of them got (and took) the opportunity to join Ben a bit further down the line.

Nick Howes reminds drivers (in a light-hearted manner) at every opportunity that he is the number one driver, and I was no exception. 'Look Scriv, whatever you've done and wherever you've been, it is what it is today mate, I'm number one.' Fair enough, mate, you'll get no dissent from me...

There were a couple of cats at the depot when I joined; a very necessary commodity, with the place being on a farm. Jaymond – as Ben called him, perhaps after farmer Raymond Bower – was a large male tabby with a lovely temperament... most of the time, when he wasn't trying to gouge Jamie Aston's eyes out. And Ellie was a black-and-white female; Jaymond's sister. I use the past tense, because sadly they are no longer with us. Ellie died on the morning of Christmas Eve 2019, and Jaymond went AWOL in 2021 during the Coronavirus pandemic!

Ellie did the hunting in the main. She would regularly bring Jaymond a meal, which he immediately devoured. That said, he wasn't averse to catching his own food supplements, because they were both well fed, usually by Ben.

As I write, we have a new kitten. She's jet-black, with the name of Cat; very original!

Over the now (almost) seven years that I have plied my trade at Select, others joined, due to Ben's gradual expansion of his business. These people included Dave Farrow (who left Select in March 2023); Gordon Brannan; Jackie Poole; Maxwell Ramsden (recently left to fulfil his dream of living in the north of England with his family. It's my dream too, to live in Northumberland).

Also joining us were Darren Stones, Lee 'Re' Turner, (so called because he left the company but returned to Select shortly afterwards - he has since left us again), Martin ('Swedge') Aston (no longer with Select; he joined JCB, Martin ('Plug') Anderson, and from January 2020, my friend and former Wednesfield colleague, Claire Wilde, who joined as Garage Manager, overseeing the later influx of former Arriva drivers in April 2021, and June 2021, when Arriva Cannock was sold to D&G. The (Cannock) depot, at the time of writing, continues to operate under the Chaserider banner, but ownership of the company transferred to D&G Bus and Coach (which Julian Peddle owns, amongst other bus companies).

I settled into the lanes duties, and still enjoy them, although these days I work the same duty on all the days I'm at work. I route-learned the 877/8 routes from Martin Elson; unfortunately, however, on our 'maiden voyage', the bus suffered a minor mechanical failure in Little Onn, preventing us from continuing our journey by the time the problem had been sorted. We did it again soon after, and I picked it up, with assistance from the notes I made whilst route-learning.

On the evening of Saturday 5th October 2019 (my eldest granddaughter Molly's sixteenth birthday), Mike Brown arranged a surprise garden party, which was held on the lawn of the farmhouse. It was to mark a double family celebration; our boss's thirtieth birthday, and his and partner Chantel's son Thomas's first. The party was attended by most of the workforce, and their partners and some family members; farmer Ray Bower with some members of his family joining the fun for a while, too. It was a great evening, enjoyed by all. By this time, Chris Kent and Jackie Poole were in a relationship (as they still are today), and during the previous year, Gordon Brannan had taken up Mike Brown's offer to join him 'on the spanners'. Gordon, a diamond bloke, went into the workshop as an absolute rookie in 2018, but to his (and definitely Mike's) credit, he has become very able and confident with his new responsibilities. As things stand at the moment, however, Gordon's work is passed by Mike before the job is 'signed off'. Over the years, there have been other engineers who have joined but not stayed too long (for reasons known to only a few), notably a young man called Ashley Munday. Ash is the grandson of my ex-wife Tina's late stepdad, Arthur Mulley. Arthur and Tina's mother Alice were happily married for some twenty-five years before his passing. A back injury caused Ash to take a considerable amount of time off work in 2021, but happily he's over the worst and back doing the job he loves, albeit for another company – we're still in touch, though. He's a good one is Ash, and he knew his job, too, and I think it was detrimental to the workshop when for whatever reason he left the company...

A little while before the surprise party, Ben said he wanted to speak to me in confidence. Well, that was no problem, because due to my past positions, and not just in employment, I have been called upon to keep a confidence on many occasions. During the chat, Ben announced that he wanted to relieve Chris Kent and me from full-time driving duties, and instead, if we both agreed, we would become 'yardmen/spare drivers'. By this time in my career, I was well beyond the official retirement age, and the oldest person in Ben's employ... so I jumped at the opportunity to reduce my (driving) hours! And Chris agreed to the new role, too. Ben told us that big changes were happening at the depot 'in the near future', and when these changes were in place that would be the time when our roles would also change. He even took the opportunity to elaborate a little, regarding the forthcoming changes, whilst his party was underway.

Chris, however, left Select Bus Services on 19th August 2020. He is now happily employed at D&G Bus and Coach's Longton depot. Ben chose Darren Stones to take Chris's place, but it didn't work out, and Darren returned to full-time driving duties. As for me, there has been no word from Ben regarding my supposed new role, other than, for a very short time, asking Martin Elson to put me on one of the two duties Darren and I shared (no.4 and no.10), which did actually include time at the yard rather than all day on the road. But even that token gesture soon ended, with absolutely no explanation. Not that he had to actually give me a reason, I accept that... but it would have been nice!

If I mention it, not directly, but as a throwaway comment, Ben's response is always, 'Well you said you didn't mind.' I have never actually said that, though; it is more a case of getting stuck into what I'm doing now.

Instead, other drivers, fresh to the depot, and a good deal younger than me, have of late been doing what I was told I would be doing. The other person now on yard duties on a seemingly permanent basis is Jamie Aston; largely, I suppose, because he took over from Max Ramsden as the company fueller/cleaner, for a while anyway. He does, however, when required, do some driving... as does Martin Elson, and even Claire Wilde, as and when the need arises – which it does, and always will. These days, Jamie is responsible for keeping the fleet as clean as possible with his limited resources; and time, because he has other work to do, i.e. banking, and driving rail replacement buses, as and when required.

We have a chap called Steve Allen fuelling and parking the buses up now.

I think it is worth mentioning that whenever Martin allocated duty 4 to me, the time I spent at the depot was taken up actually working, i.e. litter-picking the yard; cleaning the drivers' room, and even thoroughly cleaning the toilets! I obviously didn't have to do any of those tasks, because the people on the yard these days rarely do.[6] But I was being paid, so insisted on doing my bit! Mike Brown, seeing what a complete and thorough job I made of cleaning the mess room (no pun intended), asked if I would mind having a go at his office in the workshop. I obliged, and he kindly thanked me.

The Coronavirus/Covid-19 pandemic struck in 2020 and it caused absolute mayhem around the world! For us in Britain, Prime Minister Boris Johnson imposed a complete 'lockdown' from 23rd March, as and where he was able to do so. Obviously, essential services had to continue, albeit on a much-reduced level, and this included public transport. We became – as far as we were concerned, because we were never really recognised as such – part of the 'key workers' sector, if you will. Ben Brown, I have to say, was brilliant during that awful period; he provided work for every full-timer who wanted to continue working, and furloughed those that didn't, or couldn't, due to their own personal circumstances.

Each working driver was provided with forty hours' work over a four-day week. Ben's plan was a total success, and we all got through it, despite a good number of us (myself and Tina included) falling victim to the virus at different times during those dark days! We (Tina and I) contracted Covid-19 in January 2021, when it was rampaging across the globe! I was only mildly affected, but it really knocked Tina about.

We were all issued with a document (see below), which was to be handed to the police if we were 'apprehended' and

---

[6] Simon Gray-Davis has done a sterling job on the yard whilst not being able to drive due to health problems.

suspected of breaking lockdown rules whilst travelling to or from the depot:

For the attention of UK Police Officers
Confirmation of Employment in the Transport Sector during the National Lockdown Period
The transport sector is exempted from the national lockdown, including those who will keep the air, water, road and rail passengers and freight transport modes operating during the COVID-19 response.
This document is valid from 26th March.
Please accept this document as confirmation that the holder is employed by B P Brown Travel Ltd T/A Select Bus Services, and performs work within the transport sector. The employee is required to travel to and from work; and/or to buses out of service, or to change drivers, or to carry out essential repairs.
I hereby confirm that the information set out above is true and correct.
B P Brown, MD
Select Bus Services

Schools were completely shut down for a time during the worst of the pandemic. And when it was considered safe to reopen them with caution, it was decided that school runs would be dedicated to school students only; no member of the public would be permitted to travel with students until social-distancing measures were deemed no longer to be necessary. As well, a limit was put on numbers of students travelling on public transport. With this in mind, Ben asked me to do no.3 duty, saying (quote): 'I trust you to do it properly, Scriv.' I appreciated his confidence in me, so I accepted the challenge. The duty required me to complete two trips to the Wolgarston High School in Penkridge before 0900hrs, in a double-decker bus. The first journey would cover Wheaton Aston; then it would be a drive to Bishops Wood via the A5, and then on to the traffic nightmare that is Brewood, before returning to the school with the students from those villages; hard work, but really enjoyable - so much so that when life did return to some form of normality, I asked Martin Elson (as it was now obvious that I had been overlooked for the position Ben had earlier offered me) if I could have no.3 duty (which included one run in the double-decker to the school every morning, and one from the school in the afternoon with a different group of students, in a single-decker bus) on a permanent basis. The hours in between my school responsibilities, and afterwards, would be taken up on routes 877 and 878 between Stafford and Wolverhampton, either side of a one-hour lunch break in Stafford. At the time of writing, I am still performing this duty, although there has been a change in what I do. My regular vehicles during the pandemic were fleet no.17 (double-decker) and fleet no.8 (Dennis 'dart' saloon). Both buses have now (sadly) been stood down, and scrapped.

From joining Select, and right up until October 2021, my relationship with Mike Brown had been excellent. He was always willing to offer good advice if a problem with any of my own (personal) vehicles arose, sometimes even actually correcting the problem for me. At the time I joined, Mike was Ben's only engineer, due to the small fleet of buses Ben operated in service. That said, however, Mike worked very hard to keep the fleet maintained and on the road. I used to tell him that all the drivers appreciated his work-rate and willingness to help us whenever he could.

He kindly loaned me decorating equipment and ladders when I moved from Wolverhampton to Penkridge in 2017 (after a short period in Wales), and I really appreciated that. I quickly grew to like Mike, as my peers did, too. Below is a tale worth the telling here, involving Mike and me:

A couple of bottles of Bell's whisky stood on the engineers' table in our 'mess' or communal room at the depot.

Ben, knowing that an increase of work, therefore drivers and buses, was becoming ever more likely, purchased a large building (in pieces) which he, Chris Kent, Martin Elson and I think Mike, put together to make our new premises. The building is large enough to house an office for Ben; and another for Claire Wilde, as well as an open-plan traffic office space and a reception, plus the aforesaid communal room. There's even a room for Mike in there. I digress...

So these bottles of whisky (seemingly), one standard and the other a very nice-looking dark ebony variety, had not been touched for a week or two. Being someone who enjoys a drop of the old golden throat juice, I thought I would chance my arm. I asked Mike if the whisky was ever going to be consumed; or was it for sale, perhaps. I added that if it was, I would be interested in the darker of the two. Mike just smiled. It was a Monday morning, and Monday mornings are notoriously busy for the engineers as they work to ensure a full run-out. Mike was off out into the yard, but before he went, he turned to me and said that if the bottle was still there at finishing time on Friday, I could have it. I was over the moon because I considered that what Mike was saying actually meant that it would still be there!

I was counting the days. I wrote on a piece of A4 sized paper: '5 days Mr Brown' with a winking-eye face. He wrote in response: 'Yes, but it's still here'. I added 'Until the 5th Sir'. By Wednesday, however, one bottle had gone, but my bottle remained, with a further message from Mike: 'Friday pm'. Thursday ran into Friday morning; the bottle hadn't moved, and I was getting more than a little excited. I moved it from where it had stood all week, to the worktop nearest the door. I then wrote on the A4 sheet: 'I've put it here so that I don't forget it'. Upon my return to the yard, I dashed into the mess room to find, to my absolute surprise and delight, the bottle of dark ebony whisky was where I had left it.

Mike had written on the paper: 'Take it, enjoy'. I responded with 'Many thanks, Scriv xx'. I put the bottle in my bag, and drove home, delighted with myself – and with Mike of course. I had enjoyed the banter (in the form of our messages) all week, and it had culminated in a seemingly remarkable feat of kindness from the boss's dad. That evening, Tina and I were visited by a couple of my relatives, so I thought it would be nice to offer them a glass of my lovely whisky. They accepted, and I poured each of them a generous measure. Simultaneously, they took a decent slug, and simultaneously they immediately spat it out...all over our brand-new sofa. 'Fuckin' 'ell Scriv, they said in unison, 'it's cold tea, you twat!' What?

Tina went berserk!

Cheers, Mike; you stitched me up good and proper, and I deserved it!

A short while later, to make amends, Mike left me what he said was two genuine bottles of lager. It looked the colour of urine, so this time I was taking no chances. I poured both down the toilet, where it had earlier occurred to me, was its rightful place! Upon hearing of this, Mike, Gordon Brannan and everyone else present pissed themselves (no pun intended) laughing! They were both at pains to insist that the bottles contained genuine lager, but as the fake whisky bottle appeared to be sealed, I thought likewise of the lager bottles! Relations between Mike and I, however, turned sour at the back end of 2021 – October, to be precise – after a dispute occurred between Traffic and Engineering (yes, that old chestnut again) which I somehow got involved in.

We had all been clocking in and out at work, up until April 2021. I hadn't previously engaged in this archaic procedure since my first job at Carvers, back in the late sixties.

The practice of Select drivers clocking in and out stopped

when the company expanded, due to Select's share of Arriva Cannock Depot's work, after it ceased operating as Arriva. Our company took on the Stafford duties, and D&G Bus and Coach became responsible for the Cannock work; trading as Chaserider out of Cannock depot, which was sold, apparently. A man very well known in the industry, Julian Peddle (whom I mentioned earlier) had previously purchased D&G, and as he already had shares in Select, it was only right and fair that the work was 'divvied' up, I suppose. Julian also owns 'Centrebus' bus company. Talk about having a finger in every pie... or covering all bases!

Following the expansion, which brought a number of Arriva personnel to Select, as I said above, Claire Wilde wrote to every driver, explaining that the company would henceforth be operating a 'paid duty' system, so the need to clock in and out was no longer necessary (if it ever was). She also issued us with new Driver Contracts, and a Company Handbook. Our pay rate was increased to £10.61 per hour, from £8.91, to bring us in line with the drivers who had joined us from Arriva Cannock.

The drivers who joined (Select) from Cannock, and various other companies (in no particular order) included: Andy Latore, Brian Smith, Carol Crick, Graham Allen, George Hackett, John Coghaln, Josh Davies, Kalvinder Singh (another former colleague at Wednesfield), Mick Astbury, Phil Clarke, Simon Gray-Davis (mentioned earlier), Stewart Tams (who has become a good friend, and is a great source of knowledge and support to me with regards my classic car – a 1961 Daimler Majestic, which I love), Stephanie Young, Ade Duvall, Steve Westwood, John Taylor, Nick Cannon, Steve Leech, Ant Rigby...and the 'dynamic duo', the irrepressible Phil Lewis, and the incomparable David Duffy! Phil is an extremely likeable bloke who'll make a joke about anything; usually outlandish, to get a response. And Dave; what a character! I don't think there's a job or profession he hasn't tackled (he says), but another diamond geezer. After hearing that military service had apparently formed part of his previous professions, I began calling him 'Colour Sergeant Duffy', and he loved it! I called him by his Christian name one day and he reacted with: 'No colour sergeant?' In response he called me Captain. Dave left the company during the summer of 2022, however. His mind was set on his work involving mechanics, but he couldn't secure a permanent job in Select's engineering workshop despite donning the overalls and helping out during his annual leave.

Gordon Brannan's stepson, Ethan O'Sullivan, was added to the engineering team as an apprentice, and Ben's mother Lyn, a really nice lady, became a member of the traffic office team. Sadly, Lyn has been laid low recently with a knee problem, so Gabby Woodhouse (Nathan's wife) has stepped in to cover. And she's doing a good job too.

Pierre Emmanuel joined from NX, and later in 2022 Louise Smith joined Select along with her daughter, Liz Dennis.

A lad from Featherstone, Greg Cook, whom I used to take to Cheslyn Hay school (on the 71 service) a few years ago, is now one of our drivers, having learnt the job initially with Arriva.

'Bunker', a young guy (they're all young compared to me now) from Romania, joined the engineers this year.

Chapter Fourteen

Llandudno

In early May of 2018, Ben announced that he would be taking a bus to Llandudno on the Sunday before Bank Holiday Monday, and everyone was invited to join him. I was well up for this treat; a company MD being so generous towards his staff was something I hadn't previously experienced during my long career in this crazy industry!

I consider the following is worth mentioning here: whatever anyone may think of Ben Brown (because he has his 'moments' just like the rest of us), they would have to agree that he is, without doubt, one of the most generous men one could ever hope to meet.

The daytrip was apparently arranged, to celebrate the fact that Ben's girlfriend Chantel Bone-Knell was expecting their baby. I had worked with Chantel's grandmother Pat at Ward Brothers Ltd back in the 1970s. It's always nice to have a catch up whenever I see Pat out and about with Chantel.

We were instructed to be at the depot for an 8am departure, and by and large we were all seated on Ben's recently acquired 'Leopard' bus, which still had its original Ulsterbus livery. It is now, however, a full-blown member of the Select fleet; sporting its red and burgundy livery. I, like my good mate Ian Tully (a proud Ulsterman) was of the opinion that Ben should have kept it in its original (if indeed it was its original) livery. But Ben said: 'It's my bus, and I'll do whatever I like with it.' Okay, boss.

Actually, Ben has recently acquired a former Green Bus Service single-decker; I wonder if the same view will apply to that, given Ben's previous involvement with that now defunct company? We wait with interest.

Those seaside trips which became almost annual were an opportunity for us all, or at least those who accepted Ben's kind gesture, to get together in a nice informal atmosphere; let our hair down, and have a fantastic day out doing our own thing once we were set down on the coach park. During the journey on that first trip, I was encouraged to lead everyone in a sing-song, which I thoroughly enjoyed, and I'm sure most of my colleagues did too. It took me back to my years with the Longmynd Adventure Camp, when we had our own daytrips to Towyn (near Aberdovey). And it wasn't just the daytrips that caused us to get involved in so many great sing-songs; it was an almost daily occurrence, whether on Camp or out and about in the beautiful South Shropshire countryside!

Ben did the driving (assisted on that first outing by Dave Farrow, who left the company in March 2023). I had never been to Llandudno prior to joining Select, so I was one of the first to put my name to the list of people who expressed an interest in joining the boss on this fantastic day out.

In recent years, Tina, my ex-wife, has accompanied me on these days, and she has enjoyed them just as much as me and most others. In that first year, Ben's friend, and a fellow operator, Mick Murphy (Coastal Liners) pulled in behind us at a cafe on the A41 (where we stopped for a short comfort break) with a bus full of his own employees and their families. I took to Mick almost immediately, which is somewhat unusual for me; I usually take time to 'suss' someone out before allowing them into my world. But Mick is a thoroughly nice guy, with an almost permanent smile on his face; how could you not like someone like that? I can't remember whether or not he was also destined for Llandudno, but wherever they were off to, they probably had as good a day as we did. Mick's business consists of school contracts and rail replacement work, and whenever any of his small fleet needs any work, he usually brings the vehicle to our workshop. The arrangement seems to suit both parties.

I thoroughly enjoyed my first visit to Llandudno in 2018. All I did was walk! The Great Orme is a popular attraction, so I set off to have a look; I wasn't disappointed. I also walked the entire length of the sea-front a number of times, breathing in the fresh air. There was a transport show on the day, but I didn't bother with it. I was happy having fish and chips, as you do at the seaside, and occasionally bumping into colleagues for a quick chat, etc.

The journey home began quite late in the evening, after we had been refused entry to a pub because we had children with us. Some of us tried telling the manager that we would be spending a lot of money in his pub... but to no avail! Instead, Ben said we could all troop off to a chippie or takeaway to grab a bite before setting off. Dave Farrow and I went to McDonald's, if memory serves.

Another sing-song on the bus, another short stop, and in no time the bus was swinging into Lower Drayton Lane; all safely returned to the depot (except Gordon Brannan and his family, who boarded and alighted near their house), to make our way home from there. The old bus had given its all, with no complaints whatsoever.

To our surprise, Ben treated us to a second trip: in the August of 2018, he took us to Barmouth and Porthmadog during the same day! By this time, Chantel was heavily pregnant with Thomas. As I remember, it might have been better had we done the trip the opposite way round (or was it a decision Ben made at Barmouth due to the inclement weather? I can't remember). On this trip, I was accompanied by Tina, and despite the weather in Barmouth, we all had a good time.

In the afternoon, we set off for Porthmadog (or Black Rock Sands as it is also known), where to everyone's delight the weather was dry, warm and sunny. A great afternoon was enjoyed by all. Thanks, boss.

I didn't join the party bound for Llandudno in August 2019; I was busy with previously determined commitments. The trip had been postponed in May due to baby Thomas enduring some health problems.

In 2020, we were in a (first) nationwide lockdown (because of Covid-19), from March until June, so the trip didn't go ahead that year...

In 2021, Ben used one of his double-deckers (old faithful no.17) for the trip to Llandudno. Tina and I joined the group, but to be honest, the journey for me was not as pleasant as previous times, due to quite a number of the passengers getting involved in shooting each other with Nerf guns and the like. To be fair, it started on the upper deck, but it did spread to the lower deck, and more than once I was 'shot' at point-blank range by one of the kids. Now I understand that kids have to be entertained on a long journey; but on occasions the situation became intolerable! It wasn't so bad on the journey home, because most were tired if not asleep, so I did venture up to the top deck to treat the people up there to my very own version of *Alouette*; much to everyone's delight... I think!

As regards the kids using Nerf guns on the bus trips, in 2022 a situation began to fester amongst the drivers which slowly developed into something of a 'cold war', if you will. I heard that there might be Nerf guns on the bus, so as I wasn't keen myself on this, due to previous experience, I decided to ask Ben straight out if he was going to allow them to be used. I approached him on the yard; there were others in the vicinity. Ben's reply was to thank me, initially, for being straight and asking him to his face. Apparently, I was only one of two people who had the decency (Ben's word) to ask him the question that others, he said, were apparently discussing behind his back. I did say that if it was the case that the guns would be on board, I would give it a miss. Ben said: 'I'm putting a second bus on for those who want a peaceful journey.' Great!

In some people's eyes, however (according to the infamous bongo drums), those of us who elected to travel on the 'quiet' bus were deemed 'moaners'. So in an effort to lighten the mood, and in acceptance of the challenge that was laid down by Gordon Brannan, I wrote the following poem on 28th April:

The Llandudno trip was approaching fast,
But will this excursion be our last?
The boss is pissed off with a few of the crowd
Who whisper their objections, but won't speak out loud.
The gripe concerns, apparently, the use of a 'gun'
Which the objectors say, will spoil their fun!
To keep us all happy, and to end all this fuss,
Ben's kindly provided a second bus.
The "nerf gunners" on one, and the "moaners" on the other,
I'll be on that one because I've turned into my mother!
Someone said, 'let's all agree to dispel with the farce
And have a good day; one and all'.
Okay. But don't ask Ben if he'll take us again
Because he'll say, 'bollocks you can all kiss my arse'.
Oh don't be like that boss, for the sake of a few;
The rest of us all have respect for you.
So let's just look forward to our next day out.......
As long as there's NO fuckin' nerf guns about!

It didn't go down too well with everyone, but hey ho, challenge accepted, Mr Brannan.

Arriving at the depot alone on Sunday 1st May at 0730hrs, sure enough there were two buses ready for boarding. Tina had made a late decision not to join the party, due to ongoing health problems. I found a seat on the so-called quiet bus, where I was joined by a few of my colleagues, including Kalvinder Singh, Steve Westwood, Nick Cannon, Martin Anderson, Carol Crick, and their respective partners. Chris

Harvey, a former colleague (for a short period following the expansion of Select) and now back with Arriva (at Telford) also travelled with us. Nathan Woodhouse was our driver for the day; Ben drove the other bus, from which video evidence proved the Nerf-gunners on board were having a great time, aided and abetted by the one and only Gordon Brannan, who was travelling with his stepdaughter, Bethany.

After everyone had enjoyed a fantastic day at the seaside, spending it as our preferences dictated, we all boarded our respective buses and began the journey home; our bus stopping briefly in Chester where Chris alighted, as did anyone else who wanted a comfort break before we travelled on to link up with Ben and his party at a McDonald's outlet on the A41. The vast majority of people (me included) whom Ben Brown kindly invited to join him on company day-trips have always appreciated his generosity; so it would be a pity if he keeps to his decision that 2022 was the final time that he would indulge us.

Chapter Fifteen

More Memorable Passengers

The reader will be aware that I have already mentioned a number of people who have at some time during my driving years been passengers on my various routes and buses, some becoming friends. I apologise to any that I have forgotten to include. Operating school and college services, as previously mentioned, has resulted in me making a few more friends from those runs. From the start of my time at Select, some of the people who became friends – even if only on Facebook – include Chloe Rowley, Charlotte Bateman, Laura Salisbury and Ellie Jones. I knew Ellie previously, as I did her siblings Katie, Hannah and Hayden, all of whom attended Wolgarston High School, because they are the grandchildren of my great friend John Preece and his wife Susan. Also, Charlie, Tegan, Lily Sabey, and Thierrey, all from Wheaton Aston, who have now left school but still travel on my bus occasionally.

Staying with Wheaton Aston, Marje Hirst and Rose Turley have become good friends. And Evie Wall is a young lady I have known since her early years at Wolgarston; she's a lovely girl, as his her good (if not best) friend from Coven, Florrie Miles. I happened to mention to Evie that my grandson Connor was into karate. She very kindly offered to give him her karate equipment, as the club she was a member of had ceased to function. What a lovely and thoughtful gesture; needless to say, Connor was delighted with Evie's generosity, as was I. And as a thank you, Tina and I bought Evie a nice birthday present.

A few of my regular passengers from Coven deserve a mention: Paul Jackson is a very pleasant guy, who purchased my previous three books, commenting that my (late) mother was 'a diamond'. Paul has lived in Coven for the previous six years, but actually hails from the same neck of the woods as me.

There's Mick and Terry; two elderly lads who travel to and from Wolverhampton together; Graham, a Manchester City fan whom I now consider a friend. John Blower is an avid Wolves fan with whom I used to work at Carvers, in Wolverhampton. Like me, John also worked at Ward Brothers for a time.

My Church Eaton regulars included Pete Davies (another Wolves fan) and his daughter Steph; and of course, the one and only Colin (alias 'silly sally') Richards. Just up the road on the way to Bradley, there lives a nice couple; Jenny and 'Tag' Whittingham. I used to see them both regularly on the 877 service, up until the pandemic; that virus changed a lot of what we had all become used to! I still see them occasionally; usually as I'm passing their lovely house, where invariably they are waiting for me with kind gifts of vegetables whenever their garden has yielded a good crop; a truly lovely couple. Tag is a pigeon-fancier, and very well-known by many people in the surrounding villages.

A nice lady called Peggy caught my bus into Stafford (where she volunteers her help in one of the charity shops) from Bradley a few times a week; it was usually me who took her home on a Monday and Tuesday, before the service was pulled in September 2022.

Many of the passengers know me by my preferred nickname of Scriv, but more than a few insist on calling me Alan, thanks to one or two of my colleagues!

Colin Chatto, a former colleague from my time as Cannock PSM, has been happily retired and living at Whitecross (a tiny hamlet between Houghton and Derrington in South Staffs) for a number of years. Colin's position at Head Office was Commercial Manager. We rubbed along well, as we still do these days whenever he travels with me. Mark and Annie from

Derrington were also regulars. Mark is a Leeds United-supporting true Yorkshire man, but as I keep telling him, we've all got our cross to bear! In reality, I love Yorkshire. Annie is the mother of the above-mentioned Steph Davies. It is quite common for all the people I have mentioned above to be on the bus together, along with Michaela Bosworth, a chatty and likeable young lady who currently attends Stafford College.

A lady called Julie lives on a canal boat in Wheaton Aston with her husband. Julie, or 'Jules' as she is also called sometimes, boards my service from Wolverhampton after her shifts at New Cross Hospital. Whenever she does, she never fails to give me something nice for my lunch; how kind and thoughtful is that. She also supported me by purchasing all of my three previous books, which I happily signed for her. And whenever she's on board, she never fails to tell the other passengers that I am a published author, and they would enjoy my books. Thanks, Jules.

Doctor Charlotte Wiley, who lives in Brewood, has become a friend over the period of my previous four visits to her home for my annual PCV medical. She has travelled with her husband Nick (a Ranulph Fiennes lookalike, in my opinion) on my bus very occasionally, but a few years ago both of their daughters were regulars. Charlotte never fails to thank me for ensuring the safe travel of Rosie and her sister Millie.

Also living in Brewood are my long-time friends, Angela and Richard Hough. Actually, Rich was a close friend of my sons before I got to know him. He's a good bloke is Rich, and someone you would be glad was in your corner if a spot of bother arose. They have more than the average number of children, including Olivia (whom I knew – as a passenger – before I knew she was a member of their family), Hollie, Becky and Joe; all regulars on my bus. Becky has recently left school and joined the army. I wish her well in her new and exciting career. Other members of the family include Katie, Cameron, Rich and Jessica.

Two more Brewood ladies I would like to mention are Sue Edwards, who works in the Wildlife Trust charity shop in Penkridge, and Jenny Gough the lady with the short blue hair from Stafford Street are always very nice and polite and never fail to show their appreciation, especially at Christmastime. Also from Brewood I must mention Holly and Lily Haynes, who travel with me on my 878 service; not so much Holly now, because she has recently passed her driving test, and has her own transport. Holly and Lily are the granddaughters of one of my childhood friends, John 'Magic' Hughes. We are friends to this day, along with John 'Wogga' Williams; both diamond geezers who hail, like me, from Low Hill.

From Bishops Wood, and members of my morning Wolgarston school crew (as are/were all of the above mentioned), I must mention Hannah, Izzy and Scarlett. These three young ladies are best friends, in fact all of the Bishops Wood students get on nicely with each other...I think!

It goes without saying, I suppose, that not all of my passengers get along with me; a few, or maybe more than a few, can't stand the sight of me, for reasons known only to them! I have never wilfully set out to upset any passenger, but you don't have to try with some of them, and that is a fact! This type of passenger thinks nothing more of you than they do the shit on their shoes. A bus driver in their eyes is just a public servant, there to do their bidding without question! And if you happen to challenge their unsavoury behaviour/attitude, as I never fail to do because I have always responded in kind, then you are immediately the aggressor. 'I shall be reporting you, what's your name?' I reply: 'Those days have gone, but you can have my name by all means.' I might say it's Dennis Dart (the type of bus I might well have been driving); or Stan Butler, from that ever-memorable comedy series *On the Buses*. They hardly ever realise that you're taking the piss, but that is exactly what they are doing too!

I pulled up outside the Swan pub in Brewood one afternoon,

bang on time at 15:26hrs. I was due to depart for Wolverhampton from the bus shelter in Sandy Lane at 15:35hrs; this service only operates during school holidays. I decided to answer a call of nature, so after securing my bus I left it and began the very short journey to the toilets just opposite the bus shelter, where I observed a lady of mature years actually filming me. I ignored her and continued to the toilets. As I came out, she began videoing me again. I asked her what she was doing but she said nothing, although she did cease filming. I never suspected for one second that she was waiting to board my bus; I thought she was some sort of bus enthusiast... yes even at that age...

Then as I climbed into the cab, she started filming again. I swung the bus right and pulled onto the bus stop and opened the doors. Foolishly, she didn't – at that point – take the opportunity to board. I asked her why she was filming me. She aggressively pointed to her watch as she held her cell phone, then she pointed directly at me before beginning to film me again. I closed the doors, released the handbrake, and drove away, leaving her flailing both arms in the air and shouting mild abuse in my direction. At the next bus stop, I rang Ben and explained what had happened. 'Okay Scriv, no worries, if she rings in, I'll put her straight.' She did make a complaint based on the fact (well it was) that I had left a sixty-year-old lady high and dry in Brewood. 'He ought to be ashamed of himself, leaving a person of my age at a bus stop.' Ben asked her why she had been filming me and did she consider that to be ok and justifiable, bearing in mind that according to the tracking data the driver was absolutely on time both arriving and departing from the square. And just prior to ending the call, Ben said, 'Oh and by the way, the driver is a few years older than you, actually!' Nice one, boss. Ben always defends the driver if he considers, after hearing both sides that the driver had behaved fairly and professionally.

Chapter Sixteen

Accidents, Incidents, and Mishaps!

When you've been involved in this crazy industry for any length of time, chances are you're going to have your share of any of the above. In including such topics below, where I felt it the correct thing to do, I have not identified anyone (except myself), or dates, etc, unless given their express permission to do so.

1)   When we initially started services from Walsall Depot, John Morrow asked me to take a young (compared to my age) lady driver out on my duty, in order that she might learn the route, if nothing else, from me. We had just departed Walsall's Bradford Place bus station, and we were waiting at the traffic lights in our Ford transit minibus; she was standing beside me, and even sitting on the cash tray at times. Directly in front of us there was a transit pick-up truck, which was loaded with scrap. Overhanging the tailboard and dragging along the road was a length of black flexible rubber tube; like a cross between a car door seal and a cycle inner tube... you get the picture. I said to my colleague, 'Do you reckon I could drive my wheel onto that black rubber?' 'No, it's not very wide,' was her confident reply. I inched forward until the rubber tube was out of sight. 'Right then, let's see,' I said, equally confident. We waited with bated breath for the lights to change. When they did, the truck set off, but we didn't move. All of a sudden, the tube yanked up as it took the strain... We started laughing, thinking we would just pull the tube from the truck. Which is

exactly what happened... but the tube had obviously been tangled up with the scrap, and as the truck increased its speed, half of its load fell off the back, with the rubber tubing! 'Oh shit!' said she. 'Oh fuck!' said I, as I quickly put some left-hand lock on the steering wheel in order to get round the truck after the driver realised what was happening! We arrived at our destination (the Yew Tree estate) still pissing ourselves laughing!

2)   On another day, at the end of shift I arrived back at the yard to hear squealing, yelping and grunting coming from amongst the parked-up buses. And as I began walking around the buses, I spotted two drivers going 'hell for leather' in a very compromising position! They were obviously enjoying their moment of (apparent) passion, so I left them to it, as you do. It was a *pretty* awful sight though!

3)   One of the new Walsall drivers had a bit of a mishap whilst engaged in a reversing manoeuvre. As a result, the driver was invited into Mr Morrow's office for a 'formal chat'. A couple of other new drivers and I couldn't resist the opportunity for a laugh. We quickly made a cross from bits of wood lying about the yard; got a piece of cardboard and before securing it to the cross, we wrote 'I.N.R.I' on it (in religious terms, standing for 'Iesus Nazarenus Rex Iudaeorum', which translates as Jesus of Nazareth, King of the Jews). As John was in full flow, lecturing the driver, one of us rushed in and handed the cross to the driver; startling both him and Mr Morrow. 'Hang on, what's this all about, why the cross, and those initials, Jesus of Nazareth etc?' 'Oh no John, it doesn't stand for that. It stands for "In Need of Reversing Instruction"'. Luckily, he saw the funny side, and the matter ended in the driver's favour.

4)   At Wellington, one of the drivers reversed out of the depot, colliding with one of the fuel pumps in the process. The driver wrote on his bus defects sheet: 'mirrors not working'.

5)   Also at Wellington, a driver forgot to apply the handbrake before leaving the bus, and was oblivious to the damage it was causing to colleagues' cars as it rolled steadily along!

6)   Another one from wonderful Wellington: One driver, having driven one of the new transit 'Noddy' buses all day, wrote on the DGR: 'Little red light comes on the dash every time the bus goes over fifty mph'. It was the tachograph light, a fixture of trucks and coaches, and the like to record the working hours of drivers. You couldn't make it up!

7)   I was operating service no.12 when I was 'rushed' by a police car in Madeley's West End, in south Telford. The excited officer ran back to me and as I opened the door he said: 'Didn't you hear the baby?' 'What baby?' I replied, wondering if the copper was alright. It transpired that a young lady had alighted from my bus in Woodside, and completely forgotten to take with her a very young baby she had boarded with! The officer initially (to my mind) tried to blame me for the lady's incompetence; I wasn't having that! I said to the policeman 'Can you hear it?' He replied in the negative. I said, 'Well there you go then; take the baby and let me get on with my job.' Whether the girl was the baby's mother or not, I never established!

8)   Whilst in the employ of D&G at Wednesfield, I was 'booked' by a bus station supervisor in Bilston, for setting down my passengers at an incorrect stopping point. The 'Irregularity report' stated that the supervisor was 'unable to ascertain' my name. He never asked me, the reason being, he knew my name! We were friends... until I was informally interviewed (regarding

the incident) by Wednesfield traffic office. He never advised me that he was reporting me. He was suitably 'reprimanded', however, the very next time we met!

9)   Whilst operating the service (we ran at Choice Travel, Wednesfield) between the Midshires Building Society Offices, and their car park in Pendeford, Wolverhampton, I unknowingly put myself in a very compromising position. The job was to carry the Midshires employees from their cars to the offices – just a short run – and back again, throughout the day. There was a turning point just past the car park, with a large office block (with dark tinted windows) behind it. Our MD Tom Young told us that the offices were vacant. One morning, I arrived at the car park for the first run. I really needed to urinate, so I stopped the bus halfway round my turning point, away from any prying eyes on the car park. And then I got out of the cab and opened the doors; stood on the platform, and proceeded to do the business, looking behind me as I did so. Job done, no worries, off I went to wait my time at the car park bus stop. On my return to the car park, however, I had a call from Dave Wilde, the depot manager: 'Scriv, have you just taken a leak down by the car park?' 'Yes mate, how do you know?' 'Because I've just had a call from that office block you stood in front of, pissing.' 'Eh? Tom said it was empty, didn't he?' 'Well evidently it's not,' said Dave, adding, 'You've just given a show to about a hundred women!' 'Oh shit mate, sorry.' 'No worries but bear it in mind, Scriv. I'll advise the other drivers.' He could have simply told everyone that the offices were inhabited. He did, actually...and he also told them about me almost bringing the company into disrepute...all in a day's work!

10) At Wednesfield, and some other depots, it was the driver's responsibility to put water in the engine prior to leaving the depot to start their duty. Fuel would have been

topped up after duty's end the previous evening. On a cold morning, I fetched a watering can and filled it with water before proceeding to the rear of my allocated bus; one of the larger variety. After emptying a considerable amount into the back end, I closed the cover flap and immediately realised that I had emptied the water into the diesel tank! No laughing please, we've all made silly mistakes, haven't we?? So what now? If I reported it, the chances were that I would be suspended, and I didn't fancy being made to look the fool that I was by the boss of the day! So as the bus was already ticking over, I decided to take my chances; say nothing, and when the bus eventually broke down, try and blag it! It turned out to be one of the luckiest days of my entire career because I managed to get through the day, or at least my time with that bus, without a hitch. The bus eventually broke down, but I (nor any other driver, as far as I know) was suspected of any misdemeanour, thankfully!

11) My very first head-on crash occurred on the road between Ollerton and Stoke-on-Tern in North Shropshire. A car driven by a lad I had only very recently been taking to school came round a bend and ran straight into me with so much force that the car bounced back and fell in an upright position (front end-down) in the edge to my offside. Although both vehicles were severely damaged, thankfully no-one was hurt. Two female horse riders alerted the emergency services; they arrived very quickly, and immediately got to work in sorting things out. The end result was a letter to me from Alison Jones on behalf of West Mercia Police, advising that the lad had been judged responsible and suitable action was to be taken. It didn't culminate in court proceedings because I agreed to the lad attending a compulsory training course (with a £140 cost), and satisfactory completion of a practical driving assessment.

12) A second head-on collision, on the same route, and involving me again, happened not long afterwards. This time, a lady driver collided with my bus in Great Bolas. No-one was injured and the vehicles weren't too badly damaged. Approximately ten days later, I received a letter from Steve Tyrer (West Mercia Police) advising that no-one was being held responsible for the crash. All's well that ends well. I didn't tell the police that the lady had been holding her phone at the point of impact.

13) One day, whilst I was driving a bus full of students bound for Stafford College, I met with a runaway horse! We had just passed the telephone tower on Cannock Chase when I spotted a young horse galloping towards us, with a few people hopelessly trying to chase it. Immediate action was necessary! The animal was heading for a very busy road junction, which I had just negotiated with care. I stopped the bus in a diagonal position, in an attempt to at least slow the horse down. It worked; it stopped abruptly, about five metres or so in front of the bus. I turned off the engine and then got out of the cab, telling my young passengers to stay where they were. I very carefully and gingerly walked towards the horse, speaking quietly to it. As I did so, the horse's owners slowed down to a gentle walking pace, so as not to spook it. It stood stock-still whilst I took gentle hold of its mane and held it until the owners could put a rope over its head. They thanked me before turning the horse and leading it back from where it and they had come from. Upon re-boarding my bus, I was given a round of applause by my young passengers. As a postscript, I received a nice card from one of my regular students, saying she wouldn't be on the bus again due to leaving college. At the end of her message she wrote: 'I will always remember you for the horse incident'. How nice of her; thank you, Holly.

14) Gordon Brannan, whilst in the employ of Arriva, had parked up outside Sainsbury's in Stafford when a young man, the worse for drink, asked him if he was going to Wolverhampton. Gordon replied in the affirmative, but not until after he'd been to the shop. The drunk asked if he could board. Gordon said, 'Give us your fare first before I pop to the shop.' The bloke paid up, and took a seat at the back. Gordon returned to his bus a few minutes later to find his inebriated friend fast asleep. He started the engine, and the drunk sprang into some sort of consciousness; 'Are we here, driver, is this Wolverhampton?' 'Yes mate,' Gordon replied, trying to keep his face straight. The bloke got up...eventually... and staggered to the front of the bus, whereupon he thanked Gordon before clumsily alighting and slowly wandering off. Gordon closed the bus doors and observed the drunk looking round and about obviously trying to establish his whereabouts... in Wolverhampton!

15) Whilst on an 878 service, and driving an Optare Solo bus from Wolverhampton to Stafford (via every village between the two towns), I pulled onto the front of the closed-down New Inns pub on Kiddemore Green Road, between Brewood and Bishops Wood for a leak (I had no passengers, and there wasn't an office block in sight). Getting back into the cab, I started to roll out into the lane. I had forgotten to close the cab door properly and as it slammed shut, some of my cash (from fares taken) jumped out of the tray and spilled all over the floor. Being the idiot I am, I reached down to pick up the escaped coins, looking up occasionally as the bus rolled on. And then BANG!! I had allowed the bus to collide with the pub sign. And although the bus was not travelling at more than rolling pace, I managed to shatter the windscreen! I rang Ben immediately and explained what I had done... and then offered to resign. Some will no doubt be saying here that Ben should have accepted: maybe so, but he didn't. All he said was, 'Shit

happens, don't worry Scriv; bring the bus back to the yard if it's legal to do so.' It was, thankfully!

16) I was operating the 878 service out of Wolverhampton at 1101hrs. Happy that all my passengers were seated, I closed the doors and began to pull away from the bus stop in Lichfield Street. Ahead of me, the pedestrian crossing lights had turned to red as I approached. I was the leading vehicle when I stopped. As I waited for the lights to change, I noticed a couple of youths running towards the bus from Dudley Street; I thought, here we go, this looks interesting. I kept one eye on them and the other on the lights, willing them to change so I could get away from what looked to be potentially a spot of bother, though for what reason, I had no idea. All of a sudden, it seemed as if time had stood still. Then the two lads began pointing in earnest at the ground beside my bus doors. At this point, I realised they had perhaps noticed a problem and were trying to let me know. Then, just as the lights changed, they pulled an old lady from under my bus! Luckily, I hadn't begun to move away...because if I had, I would have unwittingly killed the old dear! It turned out that she had just missed the bus at the stop so had attempted to catch me at the lights (obviously assuming that I would have allowed her to board; no chance). She was a very old lady, so I went easy on her with the bollocking; berating her, though, for being so stupid because she had run into the road and tripped, head-first, under the doors which on that type of bus are forward of the front wheels! Had those lads not noticed her, it could have ended very differently!

17) On a very warm September afternoon Lee 'Re' Turner was operating the 813 Wolgarston School service to Brewood. Usually, I would have been doing this run but on the day in question I was enjoying the sunshine on yet another walk on the Staffordshire Way. The story goes that one of the students

advised Lee that there was a 'funny smell' coming from the rear of the bus. Lee stopped the bus safely before going to check it out. Deciding to take no chances, Lee informed his young passengers that the bus couldn't go any further until the engineers arrived to check it over. As things stand in situations like this, a driver can only ask his/her passengers to remain with the bus, but cannot insist. Also, the driver has to open the doors. Lee adhered to both of these requirements; a number of his passengers, however, thought otherwise and decided to alight, and began walking along Claygates Road in the direction of Brewood; others rang their parents to get collected...and some remained on board. A few of the lads decided, apparently, to make the best of the warm sunshine by jumping into the shallow river (Penk) nearby to cool off. Eventually, a second bus was brought to Lee, and he (with the few that had remained with him) set off to Brewood. Arriving at the river bridge, two versions of what happened next were offered to me when I spoke, first to Lee, and then the young students. Lee's version: 'I stopped the bus on the bridge and called the kids to come and get on. As one, they gave me the Vs and told me, in a manner of speaking, to do one.' The lads' version, led by Ethan Postles (he asked for a mention): 'Nah you're alright mate, thanks, we're staying here.' I know which version I believe...how about you?

18) My youngest son Tom was a bus driver for National Express for ten years or so, before he 'wised up' and got out. He told me about the time after a break when he went to his second bus, and saw a few people hanging around by the passenger doors, obviously waiting to board. As it was winter, Tom was wearing a warm coat over his uniform. He approached the crowd and asked where the driver was. As one, they said that they didn't know, but the bus was due out; it was cold, and they wanted to board. 'And me,' agreed Tom, 'what's he playing at?' 'Dunno,' said one elderly man. 'Sod this, I ain't

waiting any longer; come on, I reckon I could drive this thing,' said Tom as he looked up and down at the doors whilst the intending passengers were shuffling about nervously. Tom opened the doors and got on the bus, where he then began to pretend to find out how to open the cab door. 'Don't do it mate, leave it. The driver will be here in a minute, best wait for him.' 'Nah, I've got to be somewhere, mate, I can't wait any longer,' he replied as the cab door flew open. 'Got it!' he shouted joyfully before plonking himself in the driver's seat. 'Come on then, let's go, you'll be okay. I think I could drive this if I can suss out how to start it.' The people shuffled around, muttering to each other, wanting to join him, but not wanting to join him! Then Tom took off his coat to reveal his full NX uniform; almost pissing himself laughing as he said, 'Come on, I'm only messing; I'm your driver.'

19) During roadworks on and near Town Walls in Stafford, all services into the terminus at either Pitcher Bank or Gaol Square were diverted all around the ring road roundabout and then required to access Pitcher Bank by way of a one-way slip road, which one would usually drive along in the opposite direction that the road normally operated under. Some drivers had decided to exclude the roundabout and instead turn left into the slip road. The problem was that the bus would not be in the nearside lane having come through the traffic lights, because the road-works included the nearside lane being non-accessible until you had passed through the lights. So it was a case of swinging over and into the slip road. A lot of drivers, from all companies running into Stafford, should have known better than to perform this obviously risky manoeuvre...but only I got caught out! And I know right now, as I write this, that most will disbelieve me when I say that my eyes were almost constantly in the nearside mirror as I approached the turn. If I'd have seen any traffic on my nearside then I would have driven all around the roundabout, to be facing the slip road at

the final set of lights. I saw nothing at all. Then as I began to turn, with my nearside indicator on, BANG! I had no clue as to what had happened, literally, in the blinking of an eye! A silver Ford Transit van had approached on my nearside, intending (in the driver's words after we had exchanged details) to: 'pass before you turned'. It shocked me more than any accident I had previously been involved in during all my years in this crazy industry. Thankfully no-one suffered any injuries, but I was held responsible. The bus, a Dennis Dart, suffered major damage to the front nearside. I rang Ben Brown and explained what had happened. He couldn't have been more understanding and sympathetic, for which I remain very grateful. I would have willingly accepted dismissal, because I should not have been attempting to access the road from that position. It matters not that many other drivers were performing a similar manoeuvre in order – in most cases – to keep to time; the top and bottom of it was, it was my fault, even though the third party actually admitted to speeding so as to pass me before I made the turn. Mike Brown attended, and quickly sorted things out regarding the removal of the bus, which I thought was a total write-off. Mike, however, assisted by Gordon Brannan, put all his bodywork skills into repairing the bus to a standard worthy of the very best of skilled bodywork experts. Thank you, both. I would like to mention here the fact that Nathan Woodhouse (a colleague now but at the time an employee of D&G) was a rock! He kindly stayed with me during the time I was waiting for assistance. I was well shaken up, but Nath' was there for me; thanks, mate.

20) Whilst driving fleet no.19 (double-decker) on my morning service 878 Wolgarston School, I rounded a bend in Ivetsey Rd, on the approach to Wheaton Aston with the students from Bishops Wood on the top deck when BANG!! The top nearside of the bus clattered a tree branch that had come to rest across the lane, at the level of the top of my bus. There

was no avoiding it; it was so close to the bend. Fortunately, as it is a sharp left-hand bend, I wasn't travelling very fast. The hit, however, was still hard enough to take out the marker light and cause some grief to that part of the bus. I stopped a little further along the road, where it was straight. I then went upstairs to ensure that my young passengers were all okay. Making my way back out of Wheaton Aston by the same route, after picking up the Wheaton Aston students, I met Ben Brown (coming from the opposite direction) just after negotiating the branch and the bend. Luckily, I was able to clear the offending branch from this side of the road. I took the opportunity to stop Ben in order to explain the problem. He accepted my explanation for the damage and promised to contact the council to get the branch cut off. Low-hanging branches are a constant nightmare when driving double-deckers in the country lanes. When we started running these buses, Ben arranged for the council to come out and trim all the low-hanging branches; it's now time they did it again (as I write...)

21)   Jamie Aston was asked to take Gordon Brannan out on a route-learning mission, involving the Hart School service in Rugeley. Fancy asking Jamie. He once did a school service from Church Eaton when he became, shall we say, a little disorientated? No, let's say it as it was... he had no clue where he was going! He resorted to asking his young charges which way to go; huge mistake, as all of us who have ever turned a wheel with school students on board will know. They took him on a wild goose chase which ended, almost, in Newport! It probably would have done had he not made the wise decision, finally, to phone the depot for assistance.

22)   As the tale goes, Jamie picked Gordon up at his home and suggested that they go to Rugeley first; why, only he knows. So from Gordon's place, Jamie set off for Armitage; just the other side of Rugeley; so far so good. But for some reason,

known only by 'the wandering anorak', instead of taking the straightforward option of travelling via Baschurch, he opted for a route which took, Gordon says, 'at least a couple of hours'. Young Mr Aston fell once more into his own little world and took Gordon (eventually) to the start point of the Hart School service, via the A449 and the A5 and who knows where else!

23) Gordon Brannan transferred his 'allegiance' from driving to engineering back in 2018, after joining us at Select Bus Services. Whilst employed by Arriva Midlands as a driver at the now-closed Stafford depot, Gordon arrived for duty, and was given his driving documents (duty board and defect sheet) and advised as to the vehicle allocated to that duty on that day. Fine so far. Gordon made his way to the vehicle and put his bag in the cab, and then attempted to start the bus. Nothing happened. Silence. He tried again; same outcome. Well, when anything like this happens, the driver initially informs the traffic office, because the chances are he/she is going to be late departing the depot. Once the office has been made aware of the problem, the usual plan of action is to then tell the driver to advise the engineers. They would attend the vehicle (usually in their own good time), to either correct the problem or ask the driver to go back to the office and ask for an alternative bus. Gordon was told to report to the engineers the fact that the bus wouldn't start. He did so, and upon telling the engineer he approached, he received this response: 'I'm not surprised mate, there's no fuckin' engine in it!' You might think how on earth could this happen; where's the communication? And you would be absolutely right... because the exact same scenario was played out on the following morning! Gordon was allocated a bus with no engine on two mornings, consecutively.

24) Upon returning to work on a Monday morning following two weeks' annual leave, I asked Martin Elson to arrange a pre-

MOT check for my Ford Connect van. He said he would sort it (Ben Brown doesn't mind us doing this, and we employees are very grateful as it saves us having time off to get our vehicles sorted). On the following day, I used my car to get to work, leaving my keys hanging up in the reception area, as a few other drivers do. Before leaving the depot to start my duty, I mentioned to Lyn Brown that I had left a 'rest day request' form on the despatch counter for Martin (he being responsible for sorting such requests positively or negatively); she promised to remind him when she saw him. During the afternoon of that same day, I received a message from Lyn via the bus ticket machine. It said: 'Hi Scriv. Martin is back from MOT and has your form'. I immediately thought that he had mistaken what I had said on Monday, and taken my car for an MOT. I rang Lyn immediately, and in an agitated voice I said that it was my van that should have been taken for an MOT check not my car, to be tested! She allowed me to finish before quietly saying 'He took a bus for MOT, Scriv. He's back now and has your rest day form.' Not for the first time, I felt a proper idiot! Retirement? Oh where are you??

25) In January 2023, Ben Brown had cause to contact a 'Breakdown Recovery' company as fleet no.24 had developed a mechanical problem that couldn't be rectified at the roadside. Unfortunately, the very dependent Kevin of 'Coach Aid' wasn't available to recover the bus due to the distance involved (Kev prefers local runs), so Ben had to ask another company (which he had hitherto never used), that had been touting for business for a considerable time. Talk about first impressions!

The bus was loaded onto the recovery vehicle and the journey back to the depot began smoothly. And all remained very well, right up to the point where the recovery vehicle turned into Lower Drayton Lane. That is where things went horribly wrong! The bus: MX53 FEH (a large single deck 'Commander') had somehow come free of its moorings and cast adrift, if you will. It slid off the back of the recovery vehicle; the driver stopped a little way in front, obviously having realised what had happened. But in this short space of time, the bus wasted no time in rolling forward... and coming to a sudden stop as it collided heavily with the rear of the recovery vehicle!

26) I pondered for an age almost as to whether I should include the following story. And I realise that more readers will disbelieve than believe, but the fact is, it happened, so here it is: I was working for Choice Travel on the no.510 route between Wolverhampton and Perton. It was a really nice route, with decent passengers, and I enjoyed driving the fifteen-minute service which we amicably shared with TWM. One day, at about mid-morning, I approached the Sainsbury's (terminus) bus stop to see a youngish couple, both dressed in light, cream-coloured clothing, waiting at the stop. They both smiled at me as I opened the doors. Then after the gentleman asked for two tickets to Wolverhampton, the young lady looked me in the eye and said, 'Sometimes life is on the mountain, and other times it's in the valley.' The man then gave me two bright, shiny pound coins, which I dropped into the cash tray. Before I could say anything, he added; 'we told you this when you were a child.' Then after another smile, they both moved down the bus and sat together, about halfway down the aisle. I just assumed they were off their heads! But as long as they behaved, I thought, no worries, they can travel. I continued on my journey towards Wolverhampton, occasionally looking at them through the rear-view mirror, and every time I did so, they both smiled warmly. Now I have already told you that I treat the passengers as they treat me. When I arrived at the 'business end' of the route; Chapel Ash, I stopped looking in the mirror and concentrated on getting through the (busy) traffic and into the bus station, with my 'seated load'. As the passengers stepped off the bus, most said thank you, and I

responded in the same fashion. When the seemingly last passenger left the bus, I looked down the aisle for the 'odd couple'. Here's the rub: That couple never got off my bus!

I quickly looked in the cash tray at my pound coins, and the nice bright shiny ones that the young man gave me were nowhere to be seen!

'Sometimes life is on the mountain, and sometimesit's in the valley.'

'We told you this when you were a child.'

The fact is, however, they were younger than I was!

Make of that what you will!

But as I told you... it's a *crazy industry!*

And finally, a nice little story to end on: remember, above; I told you that Ben had said to Simon Harris, that he knew me, when he invited me to work for him?

Well.................

One sunny day back in 2006, when I was working out of Wednesfield depot, I was operating the 880 service. I picked up a youth who was on his way to see his paternal grandfather who lived and farmed at Top Barn farm, Bishops Wood, or at least very close to it. He was quite chatty, and very interested in talking to me about this crazy industry, but I was keen to discuss the possibility of his granddad allowing me to do a bit of metal detecting on his land. He promised to ask his granddad, so I immediately reached for a paying-in slip on which I hastily wrote my details. Having done so, I handed the slip to the youth and said that I was looking forward to hearing from him or his granddad in the near future.

Seventeen years later, in early March 2003, my current boss Ben Brown handed me a small, folded piece of paper. 'What's this, Ben?' I asked him, a little puzzled. 'Open it,' Ben replied. I did so, and was absolutely amazed to find it was the paying-in slip which I had given *him* (not knowing who he was other than the farmer's grandson) **seventeen years** earlier, when he was just seventeen years old! It was still in pretty good condition, and it now has a place in my Employment History dossier. I wondered for a long time why the farmer hadn't responded to a very polite request... now I know!

Epilogue

Setting out on my (then) required fifty-year journey through working life in 1968, I never, ever thought that it would include more than three decades in public transport. I must have passed the old depot in Park Lane, Wolverhampton (still operational) a thousand times or more when I was a child; either going to or coming from school, or even walking to and from work when I was at Carvers and later Ward Brothers. I never once considered that the majority of my employment years would be spent in this crazy industry which that old depot stood for.

I suppose I owe you an explanation for terming the bus industry as 'crazy'. Well, I suppose it's only crazy if you are or have been involved in it. I was actually hoping for a few more stories from current or former colleagues, because I thought that their input might give a greater insight into the industry, and its craziness. Ben Brown told me that as a youngster he travelled around with the drivers who worked for (the now late) Graham Martin at Green Bus Service. He added that he joined the company (once he realised that Arriva wasn't for him) as soon as he could; on the engineering side, initially. From his experiences of working for Graham, which he willingly and regularly offers an insight into, one would be correct in using the term which I have used throughout this book. Graham was one of a kind, even though I have met and known other characters in this industry that would fall into the same category. Graham would think nothing of throwing his typewriter through a closed window if anyone I repeat anyone, was annoying him. But the other side to Graham was in complete contrast. He could be the nicest person you would wish to meet. It isn't hard to see where Ben learnt his style of management from; I've yet to see him throw anything through a window, though!

The term also applies to some of the passengers every driver, at some point will cross paths – or 'swords' – with. Some could be the nicest and most amiable people to travel with you; others the polar opposite, whom if you had an inkling of how their time on your bus was going to pan out, you would never have allowed them to board! Saying that, however, no-one really knows what is going on in someone else's life, so we mustn't judge...that should work both ways, however.

Other road-users can also drive you crazy; it is almost always car drivers who obviously have never driven anything bigger. They just don't get it. If a forty-foot bus is intending to turn left, for instance, they cannot understand why it is necessary for a large vehicle (it doesn't have to be a bus) to use all of the left-hand side of the road in order to get the rear end safely around the corner without taking a pedestrian's foot off, or worse! Added to this is the need to protect the tyres, which can cost four or five times that of a decent quality car tyre.

If I'm honest, I have mixed feelings as to whether I have enjoyed my career. Maybe if I had not decided to pull out of the election for the Chair of the union at wonderful Wellington I might have won. Then perhaps my career would have taken a completely different path; a path that may have been straighter and narrower than the one I chose by entering into the management set. I had already gained management experience before I even considered public transport; I progressed to Assistant Self Selection Manager (having previously deputised for the manager during his terminal illness) at Carvers, finishing my eight years there as warehouse manager. And between 1982 and 1985 I was the manager of a tile outlet which also incorporated a Crown Paints franchise. Another addition to my leadership qualities was rising to the dizzy heights of "Skipper" of the Longmynd Adventure Camp.
So forgive me for saying that I cannot help feeling that an

injustice was committed against me by John Morrow, on behalf (maybe) of his paymasters. From my earliest managerial appointment with Midland Red, I decided to study Employment Law; I was determined to be a good and fair boss as my career progressed. I purchased all the books I could find on the subject, and read every one. Indeed, even now, I am consulted for advice by my peers, and occasionally even some of those in management positions. And this can only be for the fact that they know, and I most certainly know, what I am talking about, even if some aspects of E.L. have changed over the preceding years.

Morrow killed my progress, and as a consequence, my continuing interest in management, because ever since he did what he did against me I have not (with the exception of a short amount of time with D&G at Wednesfield) had any interest in managing again; and there have been opportunities even outside of this crazy industry. At the time I left Shrewsbury, and no doubt Cannock, there would definitely have been some who were glad to see the back of me. But to be absolutely honest, with you and myself, a part of me was happy that my time at both of those depots was brief. Both places could have never held a candle to wonderful Wellington, because they were 'cliquey', as most depots are in some degree; those two, however, were something else!

As I sit here writing these final words and trying to be positive, I am helped enormously by the thoughts of people I have met at some time or another during my attachment to this industry whom I consider have made life easier; far too many to mention them all, but they know who they are so I'll simply say thank you, which seems woefully inadequate, but be assured that it comes from my heart.

Obviously, being a manager (or assistant manager, as at Wednesfield for a time) whether that was Duty, Traffic or Depot, I have unintentionally made 'enemies' whilst occupying those positions. But if anyone reading this book considers I treated them badly or unfairly, I was simply doing the job I was being paid to do, to the best of my ability. And if I felt it necessary to issue the most severe disciplinary award, I never did so without the advice and support of IRPC, the professionals in Employment Law (during my time).

I attended all of the courses that were available to me whilst with Arriva, to gain a better insight into my job responsibilities, therefore furthering my intention and progression to be the best I could be. I remain very grateful to Peter Ralphs (depot manager at wonderful Wellington for some time during the 1980s) who saw in me and others (i.e. Ian Tully) a willingness, not only to join his revamped traffic team, but also to further our careers. That astuteness which Peter showed, and the faith he had in us started 'Tul' and me on our illustrious paths through the various positions we held over the next decade or so, which meant moving around the western network; like it or not!

That said, however, in hindsight, and even with the financial gains, and other benefits that management positions brought me, I wish I had stayed simply a member of the Wellington platform staff, proudly wearing my uniform and DD badge! And if I had, I would probably never have had to work at Cannock and Shrewsbury. It may be that I feel this way because I wasn't given the time to settle in at either depot. I said earlier in this book that I was unhappy about leaving Cannock because basically it was over pretty much before it began. And as it was at Cannock, so it was at Shrewsbury. I should state here and now, however, that my feelings do not represent a put-down to any of the platform staff or most of the engineers from those two depots. I mean the person(s) responsible for rubbishing my managerial career, such as it was!

I wasn't happy at either of those depots, as you will have deduced. I was at my happiest (as a Midland Red/Arriva employee) at Charlton Street, Wellington. I enjoyed my time at Choice Travel, and D&G Bus and Coach (both at Wednesfield), and certainly the easy-going (most of the time) style at Select Bus Services. But the industry has evolved since the halcyon days when I first joined it; and not, in my humble opinion, for the better. I accept that, and I would wager that the vast majority of people who are still in the industry from those far-off days would agree with me. Whilst the wages at some companies are agreeable, most are not; they are too low for the job a driver is expected to do these days.

So with all things considered, if I was asked for my opinion on whether or not someone should join this crazy industry, my immediate reply would be a resounding 'NO'.

Alan Scriven MBE

Printed in Great Britain
by Amazon

25282501R00116